To my
Beloved
Wife Beryl
x x x
x x
Hope 1992 is
~ Peaceful
year
Roy

Lynne Jones qualified as a doctor and worked for two years in hospitals, until resigning in 1982 in order to work full-time for peace. She has travelled throughout Europe, getting to know women working for peace in several countries in East and West Europe; and lived on and off in the United States, where she took part in Women's Pentagon Action. She has worked consistently with women's peace groups in Britain, particularly the camp at Greenham Common.

LYNNE JONES, editor

Keeping the Peace

A Women's Peace Handbook   1

 The Women's Press

First published by The Women's Press Limited 1983
A member of the Namara Group
124 Shoreditch High Street, London E1 6JE
Reprinted 1985

British Library Cataloguing in Publication Data

Keeping the peace. 1
    1. Peace—Societies, etc.—Periodicals
    2. Women and peace—Periodicals
    327.1'72   JX1966

    ISBN 0-7043-3901-3
    ISSN 0263-5135

Typeset by MC Typeset
Printed and bound in Great Britain at
The Camelot Press Ltd, Southampton

Contents

Acknowledgements

In addition to the contributors, there are many people whose help has made this book possible. I cannot list them all, but I would like particularly to thank Leonie Caldecott for her original idea and her support throughout; Margot Miller and Frances Connolly for helping me research it; Stratford Caldecott, Paula Allen and my mother Erica Jones for reading and making suggestions on parts of the manuscript; Sandra den Hartog for typing it; the Gray family for giving me a home to work in; and Ros de Lanerolle of The Women's Press for her guidance and advice.

I would like to acknowledge Marge Piercy's kind permission for quoting lines from 'The Low Road', published in *The Moon is Always Female*, Knopf, New York, 1980; the *Oxford Journal* for allowing me to reproduce the photograph on page 119; Meinrad Craighead (illustrations pp 6 and 162); Dorothy Mander (photo p 47); Paula Allen (photos pp 48, 57, 90, 92); and Leonie Caldecott (photo p 106).

This book is dedicated
to all the women
who care to act

It goes on one at a time
it starts when you care
to act, It starts when you do
it again after they said no.
it starts when you say *We*
and you know who you mean, and each
day you mean one more.

From 'The Low Road'
by Marge Piercy

Foreword

DORA RUSSELL

This book tells us, in the words of individual women, just what made them aware of the world danger posed by nuclear weapons, and indeed, by all modern arms and devices for killing enemies.

Our poets and dramatists – our history – stir us to the depths with stories of women mourning the dead in battle, while yet honouring the courage with which they fought. That men must fight and women must weep is the implacable ruling of Fate, so say the pretentious wise and the cynics. 'You can't change human nature'. It has taken us centuries to discover that the voice which makes this arrogant assertion comes only from one half of the human race. They never asked us women, did they? Our Ancestress Eve got punished for offering advice.

I was a feminist in my school days, when I heard about the Suffragettes' brave struggle for the vote. As to war and peace, like almost any citizen, I accepted the decisions of Government – my country right or wrong – just as I accepted the religion I was taught. At the University in Cambridge I started asking questions. For many of us students the example of Bertrand Russell's opposition to the war in 1915 was a great inspiration. But it was not until I went to America, in 1917, with my father Sir Frederick Black on a war mission, that I became both a pacifist and a socialist. I was then twenty-three.

When I wrote my first book – *Hypatia*, a short feminist tract – I said that men in my country had given us the vote as a reward for assisting them in the destruction of our offspring. Mrs Pankhurst and daughter Chrisabel supported the war, daughter Sylvia did not.

To me all the things that women want in the world – all the changes – belong together. Peace is the most vital. This has not usually been understood. For instance one of the most impertinent suggestions made nowadays is that, as a proof of equality, women should take their full share with men in war. In all the years when we were held in subjection, men at least never demanded that women should be soldiers. This is not to say that women are not prepared to support their men in the face of a common danger. Today, that common danger for all is world-wide war itself. Against this danger women must organise their protest and encourage men to do like-wise. It is not cowardly today for a man to want peace and oppose war; on the contrary, to oppose war, now that we know what it could mean for all human kind, is the courageous act, not the reverse.

I often say that the drive for women's liberation should not aim at making women act like men, rather do we want men to act more like women. Both sexes need to be set free from the menace of war in order to fulfil the creative purpose of living, for which we are born.

In the fifties I was associated with the original antinuclear committee and with women's efforts in the existing peace movements. It was younger members of the Labour Party in Britain, on the initiative of the women, and with the support of sections of the Friends' movement, who started, early in 1957, the Council for the Abolition of Nuclear weapons. One of its first actions was the protest march of the women in May of that year, which took place in pouring rain. It drew women from all classes and organisations, leading women and women MP's. Diana Collins (wife of Canon Collins) was in the chair, and Vera Brittain, Joyce Butler MP, Dr Edith Summerskill MP, spoke in Trafalgar Square. Women in black picketed the lobby of the House of Commons. And following a second march, with the addition of further prominent people, among them J.B. Priestley, and Sir Julian Huxley, the Campaign for Nuclear Disarmament (CND) was born, with Bertrand Russell as its President and Canon Collins as its Chairman. As its name makes clear, the slogan of the campaign was not pacifism, but the banning of the H-bomb. I was sad to see its aims so limited: neither seeking allies in East and West Europe nor emphasising the need to campaign for real disarmament and peace.

But I took part in the growing Aldermaston Marches and, when the movement began to get publicity in Europe, I urged that it should try to extend its marches there. This was the basis and reason for the Women's Caravan of Peace in 1958, which visited nearly every European country, including Russia and Albania, and received a very great welcome.

I can see that the best way to get *massive* support for disarmament and peace is possibly not to confuse people with all the demands that a woman as feminist or mother might make. But while we continue to stress the danger of nuclear suicide in war, we should begin to be clear in our minds as to the changes we are demanding. I will try to set down briefly what I think some of these are:

1) Equality, not to be treated as second-class citizens; this involves equal pay and opportunity.
2) Sexual respect – not to be treated as natural prey by men to be harassed and raped.
3) Similar sexual respect within marriage – marriage or sex partnership to imply joint decisions; free choice in love and not to be pressurised into marriages.
4) A non-patriarchal and less authoritarian society, in which children are valued and educated, not treated as property.
5) Cooperation: if differences are not to be settled by war but by negotiation, there must be more feeling for cooperation, both within nations and internationally. Within a family, a wife and mother traditionally tries to reconcile differences: women now, when working together, aim at general agreement, and avoid 'chairmanship', which can mean dictation.
6) Nearly everything in life, as now organised by men – in business, parliamentary procedure, law courts, trials, diplomacy, education – is based upon conflict and rivalry. All this would be changed by a change in values.

'Might' is not 'Right', whether expressed in big battalions or sacks of gold. Nor would disputes and problems remain insoluble if the best brains of both sexes were called upon to seek a solution, as to what is right or wrong, true or false. This book is full of the thoughts and feelings of women on so many questions hitherto neglected.

Since I began to take part in politics, while supporting the feminists claims to equal pay and opportunity and so forth, I soon became convinced not only that women were in subjection, but that their views on the aims and purposes of life and society were simply not understood. I wanted to see what women stand for finding its place in the councils of the peoples and nations.

We all dream of our Utopias. Mine is a world of tolerance and mutual help, in which we stop persecuting one another about religions and ideologies; stop sex wars and industrial competition; stop fixing our thoughts on a life after death and begin to realise together the beauty, splendour and wonder that life on earth could be for all upon it.

I am so glad that I have lived to see women, at long last, asserting not just their rights, but also the importance and relevance of the values they believe in. If the world does not listen, and change its course, there is little hope of civilised life, or even of survival.

Women reply to men who ask, 'What do you want, what are you trying to do?' 'We want to construct a new world with you, where peace and truth will reign, we want justice in every spirit and love in every heart.'

> *La Voix des Femmes*, Socialist Feminist paper, 23–28 March 1848.

Mothers of families write to us from all sides to ask what is to be done . . . Let voices be raised against the war. Let us protest in the name of humanity against this pastime of princes which causes the blood of people to flow. And women not only have the right to interfere, it is their duty to do so. Let them protest. Who will dare to say now that politics do not concern wives and mothers . . . Let it come, we will publish it.

> *Droits des Femmes*, (French weekly), on the eve of the declaration of the Franco-Prussian War. Reprinted in *The Englishwoman's Review*, No. 11, April 1870.

Men's bodies are our women's works of art. Given to us the power of control, we will never carelessly throw them in to fill up the gaps in human relationships made by international ambitions and greeds . . . War will pass when intellectual culture and activity have made possible to the female an equal share in the control and governance of modern national life; it will probably not pass away much sooner, its extinction will not be delayed much longer.

> *Women and Labour*, Olive Schreiner, 1911.

April 1911. In Vienna the women workers organised a mass demonstration in favour of votes for women. They marched in their thousands. Adelheid Popp said, 'But we also want to fight against the fact that millions are squandered on murderous ends and in setting brother against brother. We want an end to armament, to the means of murder and we want these millions to be applied to meet the needs of the people!' Feminine politics? No: Humane politics. And the time is fast approaching in which the well-being and the rights of mankind will be regarded as the highest political yardstick, this early initiative by the one half of humanity which up to now has been deprived of all rights is just one of the symptoms.

> *The Struggle to Prevent War*, Bertha von Suttner

I trust there is no truth in the suggestion that the Disarmament Committee of the Women's International Organisations is going to be abandoned. I am quite sure that [their] work has been of the very greatest value. It has been the interpreter to the Disarmament Conference of the deep anxiety of the women throughout the world that some serious step should at length be taken towards the reduction and limitation of the armaments of the world . . .

> Letter from Lord Cecil, President, League of Nations Union, to Mme Guthrie D'Arus, 5 July 1933

We can best help you to prevent war not by repeating your words and following your methods but by finding new words and creating new methods. We can best help you to prevent war not by joining your society but by remaining outside your society but in cooperation with its aim.

Three Guineas, Virginia Woolf, 1938

Although the cause may be partly physical – I am seven months pregnant – I find myself obsessed with the question of what is going to happen. I listen to the news bulletins like a drug addict and fall on the paper and read the crisis news before anything else.

I have joined the Campaign for Nuclear Disarmament, although I cannot be a very active member, as it is something positive to do. The questions I ask myself are 'Would any of us survive?' 'If so – for how long, and would we have to watch our children die from radiation sickness?' 'Given that we survived without severe radiation damage would we then starve to death through lack of help from outside as all countries would be devastated?'

'Standing firm,' 'the values of the free world,' 'our rights,' are all meaningless slogans when balanced against children's lives. As well as dying for what is good in our way of life, we should also be dying for Angola, Algeria, apartheid, and all the other blots on Western democracy.

What can one do to try and lead a happy, normal life?

Judith Cook, letter to the *Guardian*,
November 1961, which prompted the formation of Voice of Women

On 17 December 1960 in Mython, sixteen-year-old Truong Thi Bay, carrying a banner, marched at the head of a demonstration. Police shot her dead. Her place was immediately taken by eighteen-year-old Nguyen Thi Be who in her turn was mortally wounded. A third young girl took the lead and was killed. But the demonstration continued to surge forward; the soldiers lowered their weapons.

from 'Women in Vietnam' *Vietnamese Studies*, 1966

There is a mediaeval fairytale about a dream of a parent striving for her children's safety:

Once upon a time a young woman came to Paris, and stood on one of the bridges. She had been dreaming that she would get help here for her sick children. They had caught a dangerous disease and she had no money to pay for the medicine. In the dream she learned that she might save them by standing on the bridge every Thursday night. One night as she was standing at her usual place – for the third time – a merchant passed by. He laughed at her simplicity as she told him why she was standing on the bridge. 'I also have been dreaming,' he said: 'I dreamt that I dug under the tree in the park yonder and found a lot of gold. But I don't believe in dreams.' Scornful, he went away. But the young woman went to the nearest inn. She borrowed a spade and started to dig under the tree. Soon she struck into something hard and found pure gold. Now she was able to buy the costly medicine and her children were cured of their disease.

Eva Nordland
speaking on the Copenhagen-to-Paris Peace March, 1981.

Introduction

There is nothing new about women organising and acting separately on the issue of peace. In 1854 Frederika Bremer formed the first Women's Peace League in Europe. Bertha von Suttner wrote an anti-war novel called *Lay Down Your Arms* in 1889 and it became a runaway best seller, being translated into 27 languages. In 1915, while war raged, and in the face of immense difficulties, over 2000 women from all over Europe, the USA and Canada, met in The Hague to protest against the war, and form the International Commission for Lasting Peace (later to become Women's International League for Peace and Freedom). Their resolutions were used by President Wilson in drawing up his 14-point plan for peace in Europe. WILPF grew in size and strength during the twenties, promoting the ideas of the League of Nations and pushing for a Disarmament conference. From the fifties, in response to the cold war and 'Atmospheric Testing', other new organisations sprang up: The Voice of Women, and Women's Strike for Peace, to name but two. Women mailed their babies' teeth to congressmen in protest at the effects of radioactive fallout and held massive demonstrations against NATO in Amsterdam and Paris.

Nor is the linking of feminist and anti-militarist ideologies a new phenomenon. Women like Lida Heyman and Anita Auspurg in the twenties, and Virginia Woolf in the thirties were making that connection.

What does seem to be new, though, is the sudden proliferation in the last two years of women's groups that organise and act autonomously, on peace and related issues. It is this phenomenon that this book attempts to document. Many of the issues thrown up by a discussion on women and peace are only lightly touched on here: for instance, the history of various women's peace movements; the connections between feminism and nonviolence, feminism and anti-militarism; and the arguments against nuclear weapons. This is partly because other books deal adequately with the subjects, but mainly because it seems to make sense to start where women are rather than defining where we have been in the past or stating where we should be in the future. We are taking action. Some women are not making a profound theoretical analysis first, regarding this as superfluous. This book looks at the forms of action we take, how we organise and why we're doing it, in the hope that this may provide an inspiration and in some cases a practical guide to further action by others. At the same time, by bringing together the stories of different women with different philosophies and different ways of working for a similar cause, it may be possible to begin to look at how effective we are being.

Because of the limits of my own experience and knowledge the book is centred on Britain, although I have tried to break out of this insularity by including contributions from Japan, the USA, Germany, Holland and Norway. The contributions were selected because they did one of two things. They either discussed a particular form of women's action, such as a lobby, a long-distance march or a peace camp, or they discussed at a local level a particular approach to women organising: for instance Nottingham WONT as feminists, the Oxford Women as mothers. Such a book cannot hope to be comprehensive but I hope it is representative.

One might ask why there is such a proliferation of autonomous women's activity at this time. One could note the growth of the peace movement as a whole: in the sixties at its most active CND had a national membership of 15,000. In the last two years national membership has jumped from 3,000 to 50,000, to say nothing of local groups and new campaigns, such as the one for European Nuclear Disarmament and the World Disarmament Campaign. Nor is the growth purely a British phenomenon. Demonstrations in some cases numbering a quarter of a million people or more, filled the streets of Rome, Amsterdam, Paris, Madrid, Helsinki and London in October 1981, to protest against the arms race. Half a million people filled Central Park in New York on 12 June 1982 to mark the start of the Second UN Special Session on Disarmament. One could also cite the political framework in which such growth has occurred. On 12 December 1979 NATO made a decision to deploy Cruise Missiles and Pershing II in Europe, thus bringing home to people that a new stage had been reached in the nuclear arms race – a stage that embraces the concepts of a nuclear 'first strike', and of actually fighting limited nuclear wars, sited in an expendable Europe. The crises in Afghanistan and Iran added to international tension, increasing people's awareness that the world was becoming less and less a safe place to live. Meanwhile the involvement of the USA in E1 Salvador, the reintroduction of the draft, Reagan's election, and the immense increases in defence spending in the USA all added fuel to the fire. In Britain the Thatcher government opted for Trident nuclear submarines at the cost of millions of pounds, lied about the effectiveness of civil defence and daily became less able to supply the jobs and social services that people needed. Bearing all this in mind, and the increased political consciousness of a generation familiar with the Vietnam War and the anti-nuclear power activism of the seventies, is it surprising that the peace movement grew?

But why a separate Women's Peace movement? Is it because of the growth of the Women's Movement and feminist consciousness over the last ten years? Is this a natural consequence? The contributions in this book would indicate that it's not quite as simple as that.

For one thing, many note a definite reluctance by the Women's Movement to involve itself in the issue, at least initially. When Eva Quistorp tried to circulate a Women's Appeal against the Arms Race in February 1980 in West Germany, the feminist journals were not really interested. They thought 'peace was too general and emotional a topic'. Nottingham Women Opposed to the Nuclear Threat (WONT) state that 'Most feminists give the nuclear issue a low priority'. Some women feel that by working on peace issues we reinforce the stereotyped role of woman from which we are trying to escape – woman as 'mother to the world', conciliator, mopper-upper of men's troubles – an image which the media exploit. Some feel that accustoming oneself to the use of violence is a necessary part of women's liberation, and have difficulty reconciling this with the non-violent philosophies of many women's peace groups. For others it is simply a feeling that mixed groups (of men and women) are dealing with this issue, but not with rape, abortion, day-care and so on, and that therefore feminists should give these issues a priority because no one else will.

Both WONT and the Women's Pentagon Action (WPA) writing in this book define themselves as feminists who disagree with these opinions. WONT argues that 'feminism has an analysis for the whole of society, not just women's issues' and that 'feminists must make clear and act on their analysis of issues like militarism'. They see the need for women to be 'assertive' rather than 'conciliatory' peacemakers, breaking out of the stereotyped role, and they argue that the use of violence propagates a violent society. WPA argue that only by making the connections between feminism, ecology and antimilitarism, by resisting all forms of violence – to women's bodies, the earth and all living creatures – can life on this planet be

3

saved. Both these groups organise separately because this enables them to develop a feminist working process and analysis that they see as essential to preventing all violence, not just that of nuclear weapons. Their actions spring from this analysis.

In contrast to these groups there are large numbers of women who felt compelled to act *because* of the traditional roles in which they found themselves. They are women like Jini Lavelle who writes, 'We were all mothers – this is still our common bond, with a deep fear for our children's futures hanging in a mushroom cloud above our heads.' These women organised separately because they wanted to feel 'comfortable, accepted and uncriticised' and also, as Tamar Swade points out, because the role itself puts limitations on the times and ways in which they could work with others. They focussed on the single issue of nuclear weapons to avoid ideological conflicts. In some cases, as with the Women's Party for Survival in the USA, they actually avoided association with the Women's Movement for fear that 'the party would have lost its chance to become broadly based . . . appealing to the vast majority of women in this country who still held traditional views'. Such groups have been among the most active and fastest growing.

There does, however, seem to be yet another category: groups whose actions spring neither from a feminist analysis nor an emotional response to a single issue. These are organised by women with a fairly pragmatic approach who, having seen that their own sex was not getting involved for a whole variety of reasons, started looking for ways to involve them because the issue was too important to ignore. They organised autonomously because this seemed to be a good way of getting women to take action on disarmament issues, not because such actions were necessarily liberating or because they emphasised a particular woman's role. Anne Pettit organised a walk to Greenham Common because she wanted to find a way that 'ordinary women like myself' could express themselves. Dutch Women for Peace wanted to raise women's consciousness on the arms issue so that they could then go on to work in mixed peace groups.

The actions that all these women have taken reflect this diversity of approach. Feminists, determined to challenge the roots of a social and political system with which they disagree, focus on this in a symbolic or direct form. They blockade the Pentagon 'because it is the workplace of imperial power'. Or they concentrate on developing non-hierarchical, cooperative, empowering forms of group process that challenge traditional patriarchal forms of organisation.

4

The Women's Party for Survival has no problem in working with traditional forms of organisation. Indeed it sees success being achieved through *more* women learning to use these forms and getting their views across to their elected representatives. The Oxford mothers involve children in their actions, while the Greenham women were quite happy to allow men on their march as long as it remained a women's initiative.

However, this, like all categorisations, although it may initially appear to clarify, actually shows that people can't be categorised. For one thing, some women just won't fit. The Shibokusa women in Japan take their extremely courageous form of direct action on themselves because they see themselves as expendable, freeing other women for childrearing; and at the same time regard themselves as the strongest women in Japan – 'We want other women to be like us,' they say. Tamara Swade, having written, with others, a feminist analysis of the nuclear threat, then started a mother and baby group because of the feelings motherhood produced for her. German Women for Peace is so broad it seems to encompass all the differences described above.

Secondly, in spite of the diversity, it is extraordinary to see how much all these groups have in common. They all emphasise the importance of considering the personal needs of their members, or providing emotional support in dealing with a horrifying and frightening issue. They share skills and, apart from Women's Party for Survival and the Shibokusa women, appear to be leaderless, non-hierarchical and unbureaucratic. (It is interesting to note in this context that it is the Women's Party which is least concerned with its autonomy as a 'women only' group.)

In their actions too there are common strands. They talk of the importance of dreams. They constantly emphasise the positive: Women For Life on Earth, Children need Smiles, A feminist world will have healthy food, reproductive choice, etc. They emphasise the importance of imagination and use symbols in a way that is sometimes visionary – the puppets of rage and mourning at the Pentagon, the sand outside NATO headquarters in Bonn, the tree on the Greenham banner and Mount Fuji in Japan, and they stress the importance of subjective feelings as a guide to action. Indeed, Dutch Women for Peace state in their manifesto that one should not talk abstractly about nuclear weapons. Where do such strands come from? Could we build on them?

Finally, this categorisation and indeed the book as a whole tries to pin down in a static form what is in fact a dynamic process. It's going on now as I write. It was hard at times to get authors to finish their articles or leave them unaltered. Many of the women felt that taking action has changed them: Jini Lavelle states how being in the mothers' group has given her confidence and an awareness that she is a feminist. Eva Quistorp talks of German women realising the value of acting together as women and for the first time having to justify that to others. Greenham became an exclusively women's camp and the experience of living there has radically altered the course of numerous women's lives. The actions continue. Groups such as the Oxford mothers who formed to organise a one-off event found there was a value in continuing as a group. Dutch Women for Peace no longer regard themselves as a stepping stone to the mixed peace movements but as a body with an identity of its own. New women's peace camps are created, in Holland and Lincolnshire, while WONT and WPA grow in size and influence.

One cannot, out of all this, show that there is a woman's way of acting for peace, nor do I think it worth trying. I simply hope that by mapping all this richness and diversity, we may learn from each other and share our strengths with everyone else.

Women for Peace *by Meinrad Craighead, for the Women's Peace Alliance*

1
Starting a Movement: Frauen für Frieden (Women for Peace, West Germany)

EVA QUISTORP

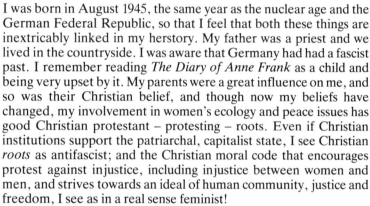

I was born in August 1945, the same year as the nuclear age and the German Federal Republic, so that I feel that both these things are inextricably linked in my herstory. My father was a priest and we lived in the countryside. I was aware that Germany had had a fascist past. I remember reading *The Diary of Anne Frank* as a child and being very upset by it. My parents were a great influence on me, and so was their Christian belief, and though now my beliefs have changed, my involvement in women's ecology and peace issues has good Christian protestant – protesting – roots. Even if Christian institutions support the patriarchal, capitalist state, I see Christian *roots* as antifascist; and the Christian moral code that encourages protest against injustice, including injustice between women and men, and strives towards an ideal of human community, justice and freedom, I see as in a real sense feminist!

I was a typical woman in the student movement of the sixties. Although feminist ideas were around then, I saw no need to organise autonomously as women. We seemed so near to a change in society then, a real change in the style of daily life. It was only at the beginning of the seventies that I began to see that we were going to have to organise ourselves. I was trying to teach, organise a trade union for women teachers, sit exams, and maintain friends and a private life, and finding it very difficult. German society was becoming more conservative and repressive at this time, with the rise of unemployment. Always at such times it's the women who feel it most. So I became involved in the women's movement, the abortion issue, organising women's centres and so on.

It was not until 1975 that I began to think about the nuclear threat. Oh, I knew there were nuclear bombs, but the awareness was like a shadow on the back of my mind, I ignored it. Then there was an action in Wiel in South Germany, when all the people occupied a nuclear plant, and I saw a slogan. It was quite simple. It said:

WOMEN DECLARE WAR ON NUCLEAR POWER
AND THE POLLUTION OF THE WORLD

but it really caught me, heart and mind. No, we are not aggressive in the male sense but we declare war, not on another nation, or race or sex, but against this destructive technology. This is the form patriarchy takes today, and it is a destructive form of power that affects everything. Look at research scientists. They have no control over what they are doing. Look at Einstein! Afterwards he says he is against the use of the bomb. My question is, what did he do before? What did these great men, who are known for their fine words, ever do to hinder this kind of science? I realised then that what we as women had to do was figure out how to combine these issues – feminist issues, ecological issues, Third World issues and the issue of freedom. In particular we had to focus on nuclear technology because it simply is not compatible with a female future.

So, I started women's and ecology groups in Berlin. I became involved in the Green party, stood as a candidate in European elections and became president of the Confederation of Environmental Groups. However I still didn't think about nuclear weapons. I knew that weapons and energy were connected but the bomb seemed too abstract and difficult to deal with, too frightening also.

It was in a typical roundabout woman's way that I heard of the NATO decision to take Cruise and Pershing II in 1979. I'd gone to a Social Democratic Party conference to listen to what they had to say on nuclear energy. A friend said, 'Wait, the next speech is on Cruise missiles.' I'd never heard of them before. The conference left me intensely depressed. How could we ever achieve anything when women were so powerless, when the radicals in the party were so weak, when the decisions were *for* nuclear energy and the deployment of Cruise? It was the right feeling to have though, because it was a real feeling.

At the same time three women were sitting around a table in Norway feeling the same way. While trouble raged in Afghanistan and Iran, they were looking for a way of turning their feeling into action, saying 'Women are capable of making a realistic analysis, so perhaps if we act together we can stop this madness'. That thought resulted in the idea of a petition: women all over the world could sign an appeal to Stop the Arms Race, and take it to the World Women's Conference in Copenhagen in 1980. I read about it in the newspapers and was so relieved. It seemed that there was hope. Those women had had the courage to be simple and direct in the face of all the experts. No, they didn't call themselves feminists – but what does this mean? To me, they were feminists because feminism is not an ideology, it has to be lived. That's what they were doing.

The next thing was that three of us got together in West Berlin – a woman from the autonomous women's movement, a woman from the peace movement (she had been president of the German Peace Society) and myself – to formulate a German version of this appeal. That we three should do it seemed very important – that the three issues, peace, ecology and feminism, should be seen to be combined in one action.

We related our appeal to the Scandinavian one but we made it more precise – in a feminist way:

> Together with the Scandinavian women, we say WE ARE DESPERATE! We realise more and more that women in the whole world are frightened for the future, and are asking – do our children have any future?
>
> Together with women of the whole world, we will turn our powerlessness into power. We will no longer continue to accept the struggle for power waged by the superpowers.
>
> When *we* talk of 'our allies' we think of our friends. We deny that men of any 'bloc' have the right to go on speaking on our behalf. When *they* say 'our allies', they should add 'our male allies'. We are supposed to ask for true disarmament from those alliances, yet clearly the interests of the military and of the war and nuclear policy-makers are directly opposed to our interests.
>
> Militarily the Federal Republic of Germany is indefensible. The numerous nuclear power plants and the stockpiles of nuclear warheads leave us in no doubt: what today is called 'defence' or even 'security' will mean the total annihilation of life in the case of war.
>
> Nonetheless, the 'strong men' continue to precipitate the crisis, and decide to increase arms expenditure. They even now plan to draft us women into the Federal army. We refuse this kind of 'equality' and shall defend ourselves against it.
>
> We herewith proclaim that:

- we firmly oppose the manufacture and stockpiling of weapons, here and everywhere else
- we shall practice civil disobedience
- we will not go into the army, neither will our sons and daughters.

WOMEN MAKE PEACE

Our real problems began in trying to get it circulated. The media weren't interested and at that time, February 1980, the feminist journals weren't either; they thought that peace was really too general and emotional an issue. And we didn't have any money. Even so, by word of mouth and by writing letters, in two months we got over 10,000 signatures. It was fantastic. Women of all kinds, old and young, sending not just their signatures but letters about their thoughts, feelings and their experiences during the war. Meanwhile three other women in other parts of Germany were collecting signatures independently of us, so that we were able to go to the World Women's Conference with 70,000 signatures collected by six women.

That was the start of German Women for Peace. We are not an organisation; it would be better to describe us as a 'movement' for which the appeal forms a common base: stop the arms race of both superpowers, remain nonaligned, take a 'woman's' point of view on these issues.

Beyond this the women are free to define themselves and act autonomously. There are many different women: older, younger, churchwomen, lesbian, radical feminists. We organised ourselves by letters. There wasn't enough money to reply to all the women who signed the appeal but we managed to send out some letters, putting women in contact with each other, and we had two national meetings to which between thirty and fifty women came, all from different towns, so a network was formed. Most women have resisted the idea of more formal organisations. They fear it would become bureaucratic, and personally I'm opposed to those grassroot democratic organisations where meetings take seven hours because everyone has to know exactly what everyone else is doing. I think groups should be creative and independent and find their own way of working. On the other hand it is a bit haphazard; we have no newsletter and no office. Communication between groups relies on the telephone, on letters and personal contact. One group compiled a book called *Women Make Peace* which has regional addresses in it. The fact that I am fairly well known is useful tactically because the peace movements and others give my name to women. The three of us in Berlin act as an informal coordination, but it's not always easy. Some women would like us to do more for them; others do not want us to do anything – they are very anti-authoritarian and want to find their own ways of doing things. That can be hard when you've had fifteen years' experience and would like to share some of it.

Actions are initiated in different ways by different women. For instance, on 8 March 1981 a women's group in Ramstien, who had read our appeal, organised a women's march to a nearby NATO airbase. 3000 women went and during the rally we simulated the effect of a nuclear attack: lying down and dying, then releasing balloons into the air with a message on them saying 'We hope you will never be reached by radioactive fallout. That is why we are resisting the deployment of Cruise missiles and Pershing II, Women for Peace.'

Another woman heard that the Nuclear Planning Group for NATO were meeting in Bonn in April 1981, so she and others planned a women's demonstration outside NATO headquarters. We heard about it and about 500 women came. It was a good action – creative and non-violent. We painted our faces, made a lot of noise with musical instruments and put sand on the ground to say 'We don't want sand in our eyes. Here is the sand of your lies about the Arms Race.' We'd also chosen a point where the world's press were present anyway, so we got good media coverage.

These actions are separate women's actions and they bring us together.

There is another way of working that is important to me, and that is in the mixed peace movements, because I don't want to stay in a sectarian feminist corner. I want to try and find ways women can enter the peace movement as feminists and create their own forms of action, and not lose their autonomy. One must always look for points where one can enter and say, 'We're Women for Peace. Why don't you do this with us?' This way the traditional movements start to realise that there are women looking for women's events and women taking action. It is hard work, one cannot wait to be invited. If there is an international event you have to go as a feminist. If there's a conference or an organising meeting you have to go. For the Bonn rally, held to mark Reagan's visit and the start of the UN Special Session on Disarmament in June 1982, I was the only woman on the organising committee. It made a difference. I fought for this picture of a woman kicking a bomb out. Now it is on 500,000 leaflets. The press releases all stated that Women for Peace was involved in the organising. Even as a little group we make our presence known.

Feminism is about being creative. We have to be clever, realise where we are discriminated against and find ways to be effective without wasting our energy. If a rally is already organised and the world's press is there, we can use it – not start from scratch every time.

I think the Women's Peace Movement is becoming an important social movement, and provided we are creative and tolerant we can be very effective. However, there are problems. The women in the movement are so very different and they don't always understand one another. The first women to sign this appeal were not feminists, but they are becoming so. This is the first thing they have done together as women, the first time they've gone out in the street as women and had to justify themselves to their husbands or their organisations. Maybe they are not so ideological; maybe they avoid the term 'feminist' because of prejudice but they know there are advantages in staying together and acting as women. However, there are many radical feminists who, although indifferent at the beginning, would now claim this movement as their own and are not tolerant of women with different life experiences. The Women's Movement was at a low ebb when we began Women for Peace and I feel if we really are going to be effective and create a new way of living, we have to combine our strengths.

This is one problem. The other is that as with any popular and open social movement there are political groups who would like to take it over, particularly those parties on the traditional left. Our non-authoritarian politics and our ideology that says 'think with your heart' sometimes make us very open to manipulation. Sometimes we are very naive. Take for instance the debate over the 'No SS20s' slogan for the peace march to Vienna. The more traditional left-wing women claim that this is 'anti-communist' and that we sound like Reagan, so we should drop the slogan and be opposed only to Cruise and Pershing. I think it is the SS20 and all the other nuclear weapons in the USSR itself which are anti-communist, and that it is essential we make a new feminist non-aligned politics that is not co-opted by any group, East or West, Left or Right. We had a similar conflict over the imposition of martial law in Poland. Some of us felt this was a significant moment that we had to use as Women for Peace. We could have reached German housewives who felt strongly about Polish women and shown them that it was not just the right wing who supported Solidarity but a non-sectarian unaligned group of women working for peace. Others felt this was not important and that it was better to avoid difficult issues for the sake of 'peace'! Sometimes these sectarian differences cause women to leave. They write or they do research but they are no longer actively involved because it is so tiring.

I don't know what will happen. I gave up my job as a teacher two years ago because I was exhausted and wanted to try other things. I didn't realise that Women for Peace would take every moment of my time. But it is important. I want to work for a Nuclear-free Europe, East and West, and I want us to create an international broad feminist perspective that is free of the 'bloc' logic and open to many kinds of women. So I will stay working in Women for Peace. It is a way of bringing different traditions – ecology, feminism, human rights – together. The nuclear holocaust would equalise everything – humans, cultures, animals, all equal in obliteration – and against this sort of equalisation we have to struggle with all our different strengths, different cultures and traditions, defending them and mixing them in new ways to make a new life.

2
Organising at the Grassroots: Vrouwen voor Vrede (Women for Peace, the Netherlands)

FROUKE SMID

Introduction

My name is Frouke Smid. My age is 34. I studied linguistics and Dutch literature in the sixties. At that time, I became deeply involved in political issues such as the Vietnam war, Cuba, Southern Africa and later, Chile. I took part in a lot of marches and other activities in Groningen, the town where I was living and studying. Slowly, the group I was in radicalised in a leftish-dictatorial way (there is no other way of putting it). There were people in it who wanted power, and took it by installing a kind of 'code': if you did not submit to this way of thinking, acting or living, you'd better leave.

So I left . . . and married, which only proved them right (so they said). I got a job as a teacher in a secondary school, which I kept for five years. I enjoyed it very much, although it took up so much time that there was nothing left over for political involvement or hobbies. Also, we had bought an old farmhouse in the countryside which we took two years in rebuilding. Of course I stayed politically interested but I did not do anything except vote now and then, most of the time for a small radical left party here in Holland, called the Pacifist Socialist Party, and I demonstrated, here and there, against the dumping of nuclear waste.

After six years Eddy and I decided to try and have a baby. Edzo was born in 1975. He is seven years old now and has been a conscientious objector, on principle, since he was four and a half. It was then that Edzo discovered things like 'war' and 'soldiers' and, as far as he could understand those things, he thought it was pure nonsense to let others fight your battles and do the dirty work for you. He thinks that if a 'king' (meaning government) wants something another 'king' has, then they should talk it over or fight about it themselves. I honestly must say that he figured this out for himself. The only thing he asks of us is to support him in these ideas later when he will be expected to be a soldier himself. The only thing we hope is that he will stick to his principles then. So much for our son! Two years later, our daughter was born.

As time passed we were becoming very frustrated with the gap between the way we had chosen to live, the energy invested in that, and the way the world is 'ruled'. Sometimes it gave me nightmares. Sometimes it filled me with outrage: why should we try to make something good out of our lives when 'others' were constantly trying to destroy everything? I could not look at anything beautiful any more (be it a painting, a building, a flower, a book, the sun, our children) without thinking, 'Oh boy, why do we want to spoil it . . . why is mankind so cold?' and, 'How is it possible when the earth is so rich, that so many people are so poor?'

What could I do?

Then I read a small article in a women's journal at the dentist, about Women for Peace. Eureka! At last a movement to link weapons and hunger, materialism, egotism and want of power and all the things that are wrong in this world.

I immediately wrote a letter and from that moment, I was involved in Women for Peace (February 1981).

I divide my time between the children and Eddy, the garden, Amnesty International, producing the village players in their annual play (which I have done for five years now) and Women for Peace. I sometimes think I am going crazy, but at least I *do* something about peace. The other things I maintain just to keep on living, now, so if I am not actually a full-time fighter for peace, in fact I feel like one. Everything I do in my life has, in one way or another, to do with it.

In the autumn of 1979, five or six women were sitting together in Amersfoort talking about the madness of the nuclear arms race. At that time the Dutch Interchurch Peace Council were organising their annual march to the NATO airbase at Soesterberg, as part of a Peace Week. The women were thinking how good it would be to involve other women, but weren't sure how. Then they thought of the demonstration. None of them had been on one before, so they decided to do it together with a common logo: WOMEN FOR PEACE. That was the beginning, and I think something like that probably happens every day to other women: they find each other, start acting together and thanks to this togetherness, feel strong.

In spring 1981 there were 400 Women for Peace; in spring 1982 more than 5000! While at the same time Aline Boccardo started a movement in Switzerland and Bodil Grae in Denmark, so we have the beginnings of an international movement.

What is it?

Women for Peace grew from the idea that we should no longer be silent about the development, production and deployment of weapons of mass destruction.

We are a meeting place for women of different backgrounds, political views and ways of life, but in common we think that:

–   the possession of nuclear arms includes the willingness to use them;

–   the possession of nuclear arms also includes the risk of using them by accident, by misunderstanding, miscalculation or misuse;

–   the system of the balance of terror does not bring safety in the long run. A war with nuclear weapons does not leave much life on earth;

–   one should not talk abstractly and rationally about nuclear arms and the suffering they will cause. Nuclear arms destroy, mutilate and kill people on a large scale. Women will give birth to mutilated children till at least the third generation. Suffering carries on. WE DO NOT WANT TO BE DEFENDED by weapons which can cause this kind of suffering;

–   differences in economic and political ideas do not automatically make an opponent into an enemy;

–   too much money, resources and scientific expertise is used for armaments. We would be better using it for education, solving the hunger problem, healthcare and so on;

–   the arms race increases mistrust and fear between East and West.

For all these reasons we want to be women for peace, as a signal that we want another kind of society, another world. We want a future for all children in the world, we feel responsible for the generations after us.

We use the Declaration of Human Rights as a basis for consciousness-raising. This declaration exists not just for those in the West but for everyone in the world. We should also consider the risks of nuclear power and the way it threatens international safety.

We are trying to change our feelings of powerlessness into protest. We no longer listen to the governments and experts who

tell us they're acting in our best interests. We think their way of thinking is destructive. We want to find another way of thinking and living, that puts pressure on our political representatives. We want women to sit and think together, about the world, about questions of war and peace, and then to fight for peace in our women's way, together with like-minded men.

How Does it Work?

I will describe how we work, using the experiences of my own group in the northern part of Holland. As far as I know other groups work in a similar fashion. There was a women's festival in November 1980 in our town, Groningen (which has a population of about 175,000). One woman, Lucy, organised single-handed an information stall on Women for Peace. A lot of women showed interest, enough to get a group of six women together who asked themselves: what can we do? They decided to start with a letter to all the women's organisations in the area (about 120), explaining who they were and what they hoped to do. They offered to do talks on the Arms Race, Women for Peace and so on, though none of them had had previous experience. So they provided themselves with publicity material from the national group in Amersfoort: buttons, stickers, etc. They read and talked a lot together on the subject. Two of them attended lectures at the Polemological institute. Then the answers came, luckily not from all 120 organisations at once! So they started lecturing, always in twos to give each other support (a good method, we still use it). They started a newsletter for interested women and advertised a postbox and telephone number which could be rung for information. The phone rang constantly; it still does. Sometimes it is women who just want to say how glad they are we're doing something, or that we make them feel less isolated, thinking about the future of their children and the world, sometimes they ring to say they liked the last newsletter, or older women ring who've been in peace movements before. Sometimes it's women who want to do something. Thea takes the calls, because she's mostly at home. She takes her time with everyone. Near the phone she has a town map so that when she gets a woman from a quarter where there are no Women for Peace she asks this woman to become a contact for others. As she gets more calls from the same district she puts them in touch with the contact. When she has collected six women, she makes an appointment to go over and help to start a new group of Women for Peace.

We now have ten groups in Groningen, fifteen in Groningen Province, 16 in Drent Province and two in Overijssel, a town more than 100 km away. A lot of work has been done. Eventually of course it became too much for six women so they invited others who liked organising to join them, and reorganised themselves. Each of the original six took on one of the tasks which had become important: newsletter, setting up groups, giving lectures, taking actions, studying the subject, finances. They each formed a task group and the six women continued to meet regularly to coordinate. They also sent a representative to the national coordinating group in Amersfoot (see diagram in Campaigning section).

Meanwhile we organised an action. Lucy had the idea. We made a chain letter. Each woman who received it was asked to send one letter to Kurt Waldheim and one to us (which was directed to our own government) in which she expressed her anxiety and anger about the Arms Race; furthermore she was asked to send five copies of the chain letter to five friends. We started in March 1981. At first the letters came slowly, then they came faster and faster. We had two special chain letter women, who opened and sorted all the letters, because there were numerous personal contributions – including poems and drawings, which we later made into a book.

In cooperation with Women's International League for Peace and Freedom, we made the chain letter international and even

DEMONSTRATIE

I.K.V., Pax Christi, Samenwerkingsverband Stop de N bom, stop de kernwapenswedloop, Vrouwen voor Vrede, Vrouwen tegen Kernwapens, 't Kan Anders, Kerk en Vrede, Vereniging Dienstweigeraars, Zwaarden of Ploegscharen, Centrum voor Geweldloze Weerbaarheid, Doopsgezinde Vredesgroep, Quaker Vredesgroep, Werkgroep voor de Vrede, Stichting Voorlichting Aktieve Geweldloosheid, PvdA, D'66, PSP, PPR, CPN en VVDM

AMSTERDAM, 21 NOVEMBER MUSEUMPLEIN, 13 UUR

GEEN NIEUWE KERNWAPENS IN EUROPA

ORANJE NASSAULAAN 51, 1075 AK AMSTERDAM
GIRO 8562 T.N.V. ORGANISATIECOMITE 21 NOV., AMSTERDAM

impressed the Disarmament Committee at the UN. It was translated into Esperanto, and in Groningen we got letters from Nigeria, India and Bulgaria. By October 1981 we had 53,000 letters, so we decided to take them personally to our Minister of Defence. We went by train: 25 women all dressed in white with our blue logos on our umbrellas, bags, backs and everywhere we could think of. We informed the press, who gave us good coverage. At the Hague we asked the minister if he had read the report of the first Special Session on Disarmament, and when it would be translated and published in Holland? (This was one year after the report came out!) He replied that, 'No, he hadn't,' and that 'the government couldn't afford to translate it'. We told the press about that too, and that some Women for Peace had translated the conclusion. Later one of the Peace Studies institutes translated the rest (at last!).

In October we invited Drs Helen and Bill Caldicott to Groningen. Five hundred people, women and men, including many public health service workers, came. Then we were invited to help organise the big march in Amsterdam on 21 November 1981, to which 400,000 came. It took a lot of energy, but we went on with our grassroots work as well. The big actions have made it easier because we are 'known' in this part of the country. We produced a leaflet about writing to your MP, which has been widely used.

We help run a Peace Information Shop in the city, with other groups. We are trying to start a monthly Peace Cafe, like Women for Peace in Amsterdam have done. We think it important that women should be able to meet regularly to exchange ideas and encourage each other. Meanwhile, we all meet biannually. The contact women from groups in each district also meet regularly, and one of them attends the coordinators meetings so that communication is as good as possible.

The women in Groningen and Drente decided to mark 24 May 1982 as an International Women's Day for Disarmament. We involved 40 other towns and set up a peace camp at a NATO airbase near Amsterdam.

The local groups are busy at present trying to get their district councils to declare themselves nuclear-free. Sometimes successfully, sometimes not, but the experience in political lobbying is good for us. We made contact with the Greenham Common women and petitioned Newbury District Council not to evict them. Some groups are busy with peace education. They want to give lectures in schools, or find out what teachers themselves are doing. Other groups are studying nonviolence and alternative defence, hoping to share their knowledge with the rest of us later.

As to what kind of women we reach – no one has seriously studied it – but my own impressions are that we reach all ages from 16 to 76, but mostly middle-class. In Groningen there are many women teachers involved. The truly conservative women stay away, believing we are either paid by Moscow or too 'feminist'. We have been discussing how to reach women in factories, but haven't solved the problem yet. However, we're not pessimistic because we think we've done very well in a short time.

Problems and Conclusions

A movement growing as fast as ours has problems. They are to do with identity, organisation and communication. We didn't start out to be another Peace Movement, but simply a consciousness-raising movement from which women could filter into mixed peace groups. But as we grow, it becomes evident that most women who get involved want to stay and be a 'Women's Peace Movement'. So we have to choose. Do we want to be one or the other, or try to combine both? We're discussing it at present, and most of the women I know would prefer to try and combine consciousness-raising and being an autonomous movement. Therefore, we will have to think about our identity: we mustn't be too 'hard' or limited simply for the sake of agreement, nor too 'soft' or vague, or we could lose many of the more active women. It should be possible to speak as a woman for peace on one occasion and for 'Women for Peace' on another. This means we need good quick communication. We are developing telephone circles (see p 132–133, in Campaigning Notes). Things like this require active involvement and training, but they can work. It is an excellent system when one wants the opinion of as many women as possible, as quickly as possible, or when fast decisions are required.

It will take time to grow into a big movement that isn't rigid or hierarchically organised, but we think it's worth the time and trouble. If we keep growing as we have done, if we keep in mind our aims and goals, then we could become a dynamic movement of great power which no one could put aside or deny – and that's what we want, isn't it?

3
Working as a Group: Nottingham Women Oppose the Nuclear Threat

NOTTINGHAM WONT

How this Chapter was written

This chapter was written by the Nottingham Women Oppose the Nuclear Threat (WONT) group. An important part of our working is the sharing of responsibility and power, so we decided that the writing of this chapter should be the work of the whole group. After we had determined the areas we should cover, each of us prepared and led a discussion on one area. So although the final writing was done by one woman, what follows comes out of the shared ideas of the whole group. We write mainly from our own experience, but sometimes try to relate this to other WONT groups.

Nottingham WONT started as a women's group against nuclear power. Some of us had been involved in a mixed Safe Energy Group, which was a lively and successful group for a while. But when energy began to fade, we realised our frustration with male ways of organising, and although we tried to change the way the group worked, it seemed impossible to generate energy.

The group had been large, but only a small number came regularly. As the meetings got smaller the men responded by concentrating more on getting the work done 'efficiently'; no time was taken to look after the health of the group and its members. The pressure grew worse as the group declined. The men involved were not obviously dominant: but though open to change, they neither saw the need for it, nor wished for it to occur. Women in the group tended to use a disproportionate amount of their energy facilitating the meeting, and taking care of group dynamics – i.e. their traditional servicing role. Within the women's group, however, sensitivity to how the group is working, and how members feel is shared by all. There is a realisation that time spent in making sure everyone is involved, listened to, and cared for generates energy for the tasks in hand. We have also found it easy to work together because we share so many common assumptions about feminism.

There were also women who felt intimidated by the issue, particularly the technical aspects of nuclear power, and needed a supportive group in which to gain confidence. When the proposal to site American Cruise missiles in this country renewed our fears about nuclear weapons, we felt we could not separate the civil and military aspects of nuclear technology, and so became a WONT group.

As our group has evolved, another motive for meeting as women on the nuclear issue has become important – that is, the need to develop a specifically feminist analysis of nuclear threat, and to show the links between women's oppression and nuclear technology. We feel that feminism has a particular analysis of the structures and causes of all violence (not just the 'women's issues' of sexual and domestic violence), and of the changes necessary to remove it. We identify the primary source of violence as gender structure in the individual, in families, in societies, and believe that while society remains deeply sexist, no peace movement can win long-term substantial victories.

We don't think that women have a special role in the peace movement because we are 'naturally' more peaceful, more protective, or more vulnerable than men. Nor do we look to women as the 'Earth Mothers' who will save the planet from male aggression. Rather, we believe that it is this very role division that makes the horrors of war possible. The so-called masculine, manly qualities of toughness, dominance, not showing emotion or admitting dependence, can be seen as the driving force behind war; but they depend on women playing the opposite (but not equal) role, in which the caring qualities are associated with inferiority and powerlessness. So women's role in peacemaking should not be conciliatory but assertive, breaking out of our role, forcing men to accept women's ideas and organisation, forcing them to do their own caring. Women have for too long provided the mirrors in which men see their aggression as an heroic quality, and themselves magnified larger than life. Nuclear technology is built on the arrogance and confidence of mastery (over nature as over women) which this has fed.

Ours was one of the first WONT groups. Other groups started from similar frustration with mixed groups, or from a Women's Anti-Nuclear Conference that was held in 1980. Many new groups have started over the last two or three years, as the disarmament movement has grown, and women have wanted to work on peace issues as feminists and to develop a perspective linking feminist and anti-nuclear consciousness. Some groups are growing; they value involving more women, even if not regularly. Other groups are closed, valuing consistency, and the building of trust and confidence within the group. Nottingham is an open group, and we welcome new members, but we do expect them to come fairly regularly. Our working style demands a high level of participation and commitment, both in meetings and in activities. So it is not an easy group to join, although we place a lot of importance on being friendly and supportive.

WONT groups are specifically feminist, so they could not by themselves constitute a broad-based mass women's anti-nuclear movement. Most of the women involved in WONT are also involved in the women's movement, and many have an 'alternative life-style', living in shared households, not having a 'straight' job, etc. However, we want to reach all kinds of women, and to do this, we have tried giving talks to women's groups, running workshops, doing street theatre, etc. Our aim is to help create a broad-based women's peace movement of which WONT would be an autonomous part.

So, although we draw our energy from our women-only group, we are happy to work with non-feminist or mixed groups. WONT nationally keeps in touch with other women's peace movements, such as Women for Life on Earth, Women's International League for Peace and Freedom, Voice of Women, through the Women's Peace Alliance. At a local level, we work with Nottingham CND, although we remain an autonomous group. We usually support its initiatives and major campaigns, so the focus of our activity has been influenced by its decisions. For instance, in summer 1981 we put a lot of time and energy into organising the erection of the stage and the booking of stage performers for the local peace festival. In turn, we have influenced the local group. Two of us go regularly to its meetings, and have spoken to encourage more equal participation by all who attend. Some of the most involved members of Nottingham CND are sympathetic to libertarian/feminist ways of organising, and the group does not use rigid, formal meeting structures, preferring if possible to break into smaller groups for discussion. We have also influenced the forms of protest used by NCND and the neighbourhood groups within it. Our approach to actions is close to that of the nonviolent direction action wing of the national movement, and we use street theatre, striking symbolic actions, and music, rather than mass demonstrations and rallies.

People value this kind of contribution to large events, and some of our ideas have been taken up by other groups. Recently, there has been a lot of interest in nonviolence training, and we have been able to offer short training sessions to help people improve their meetings, and prepare for campaigning and direct action. But although our working methods and actions have met a good response, we have not begun to get our analysis across. This is partly because we have not worked it out fully ourselves – discussions around this are an important part of our meetings.

We don't want to lose sight of the issue of nuclear power. We think that nuclear power and nuclear weapons are bound together, both in terms of the technology, and in terms of the values that produced them and the kind of society they are leading to (e.g. centralisation, tighter security). Nottingham is close to one of the areas named in the government's programme of exploration for nuclear waste disposal sites. We worked with the Safe Energy Group to organise a demonstration and lobbying of councillors, which resulted in local councillors refusing planning permission for test drilling. This led to a Public Inquiry, and we put a lot of energy into organising 'People's Inquiries' at several places near the proposed test sites. These were public meetings to which we invited local people to come and find out about the proposals, and to voice their views. We wanted to stress that a Public Inquiry would not inform 'the public' or take account of their opinions, especially since the terms of the inquiry were to consider only the proposal to drill the bores, and not the implications for later burial of nuclear waste. Not many people came to these meetings – the idea would work much better from a base on the street, but we had to do it in November! However, we made useful contacts for starting up local groups to oppose the test-bores. Shortly after this, the government called the programme off. This must partly be due to the strength of opposition (much greater in other places than in our area). But we are afraid they will restart the progamme and reactivate the Public Inquiry at a later date, leaving us little time to prepare a campaign against it.

WONT is a decentralised organisation. Local groups are autonomous and very varied. WONT exists nationally through national gatherings once or twice a year, regional meetings, personal contacts and an occasional newsletter. There is a national contact address, and groups take turns at answering mail. We have a telephone tree for urgent messages. Nottingham WONT meets weekly, and we often see each other during the week as many of us live or work close to each other. (This creates problems for new women joining the group who are not in that particular community.) There are no 'officers' but we take turns to facilitate. This means preparing an agenda, seeing that we stick to the point in discussions, are working reasonably efficiently, and that everyone gets a chance to contribute. It's an easy job in our group, for everyone is aware of these things; so the facilitator just had to be a bit more aware, to notice the time, to sense we are nearing a decision. We reach decisions by consensus. If we cannot reach a decision, it is usually because we are all unsure, rather than because different women hold irreconcilable views. We usually approach decisions by a general discussion, and then let each woman say what she thinks to see if there is general agreement. If one woman disagrees with a generally held view, then we try to see if any accommodation can be made to satisfy her as well. We will postpone a decision to another meeting if the discussion goes on a long time without getting anywhere.

We have found nonviolence training tools very useful in our meetings. These are structures which help to generate ideas, focus thoughts, or improve the feeling and communication in the group. For instance, a good way of getting ideas is a 'brainstorm', when for a specified short time women call out whatever ideas they have on the subject (however silly they might seem). For instance, we brainstormed ideas for things to do to mark International Women's Day for Disarmament. All the ideas are written down without comment. At the end of the time, the list can be worked through to decide which ideas to follow up and how. We have also used strategy planning tools to try to work with a long-term perspective, and not just to react to external events. And we frequently sing or play a silly game. It's wonderful how moving around and laughing freshens flagging energy and helps the group work together. It's definitely not a waste of time. Sometimes there's a lot of good energy at our meetings, sometimes we're tired, or not many women come, and we feel low. But we always generate good feelings about each other and this usually means that our meetings can actually give us energy instead of draining it, as most meetings do. Enjoying ourselves together is important to us. We sometimes have a meal together, or go on a camping weekend.

Because we think it is important, we are all aware of how the group is working, and where it is going wrong; and we have some idea of how to put it right. There are different levels of experience and confidence within the group, especially when it comes to tasks like addressing a meeting or giving a radio interview. This was especially acute at the beginning of the group, and we tried to deal with it by sharing knowledge and skills in self-education sessions. Now, we help each other by working in pairs so that the less confident can learn.

We have done a variety of things to try to get more people, particularly women, to think and act about the nuclear threat. We have done a lot of street theatre: we enjoy working out the ideas and 'performing'. For us, it had become an easy way to reach people without great expenditure of energy and time. But on its own, it is unsatisfactory; it has to be part of an on-going campaign. Our other activities include organising events and demonstrations, running workshops and giving talks. We want to prepare a slide show to make our presentation more appealing.

It is very easy to be so involved in the constant business of organising activities that we lose sight of what it's all for, forget our long-term aim. When we have the confidence to be visionary, our goal is a feminist society. Our intermediate aim is nuclear disarmament, which we see as coming about through a grass-roots movement, which will force governments to respond to it, and through the expansion of nuclear-free zones.

How does this lead to our long-term goal? Nuclear weapons are an expression of the twisted values of a male-dominated society, but will stopping the siting of Cruise missiles bring a feminist society closer? Our answer is that it depends how we organise to oppose nuclear weapons. First, if we can make clear the links between nuclear weapons and male domination, then people will appreciate the destructiveness of sex-role stereotypes and the oppression of women. Second, if our campaign stresses grass-roots organisation and equal participation in decision-making etc., people will experience their own power, and demand more autonomy: this would threaten the hierarchical, centralised structures that are an expression of and a support for male domination.

We spent some meetings discussing our 'strategy', using some nonviolence training strategy tools. We 'brainstormed' a list of possible intermediate objectives for the group, and then each of us tried to write them down in order of priority. From sharing our lists and discussing our priorities, we were able to set down fairly precise objectives. These were:

First: to help build a women's peace movement, that would reach and involve a wide variety of women: to begin by aiming at two groups: especially feminists, and women who spend most of their time at home.

Second: to prepare ourselves for direct action, by specific nonviolence training, and by generally building group trust.

Third: to work with the mixed peace movement, to influence its working style and actions, and to try to explain and win acceptance for our feminist analysis.

Fourth: to continue educating ourselves on factual matters, and developing our ideas through discussion.

We have tried to keep these aims in view, but still get diverted by dates and issues that come up which we feel we must respond to. Our first aim is perhaps the most elusive. It is really a long-term aim, and we have not yet found a good way of contacting women outside the peace movement.

We believe that change must come from the bottom up. So there are no quick ways of imposing our utopias on others. We see radical changes in the way we live coming about as people reclaim control of their own lives, refuse to cooperate with the hierarchical structures which dominate and demean them, and create new ways of relating based on self-reliance and cooperation. Women are very important in the process. Our present hierarchies are based on the need to control and feel superior. The model for this is men's domination of women. The division into master and servant, success and failure, 'victim and executioner', is based on the division into sex roles. Women's resistance to our assigned role is essential. Women too have a different consciousness. Although we have believed in our own passivity and helplessness, few of us are really taken in by the male heroic values. Moreover, women have less vested interests in the present system, and are more easily able to criticise it.

The arms race and women's oppression are for us very clearly linked, and WONT is important to us as individuals as the only group that makes that connection. The growth of the arms race is frightening, and the growth of the peace movement can be alienating as well as exhilarating. Within WONT we are able to give each other support and work in a way that gives us energy and confidence. We feel less isolated in our thinking.

Many of us need WONT in relation to the women's movement too. WONT brings together nonviolence and feminism as no other group does. Some women condone violence against men. Others, who feel it is wrong, are made to feel that they are 'soft', 'wet' or playing the female role. WONT tries to provide an analysis to show why our opposition to male values has to be nonviolent. Put simply, if we use violence to bring change, then that violence will live on as part of the new society we create. Nonviolence also provides the methods that can make our opposition forceful and determined without resort to violence.

We see nuclear weapons and nuclear power as particularly horrendous results of male domination. We feel ourselves to be an integral part of the women's movement; as a group and as individuals. We are all involved in other women's groups, and we meet at the Women's Centre. We would like more support from the women's movement, but although we are accepted, most feminists seem to give the nuclear issue a low priority. Many of them are already involved in longstanding, specifically women's-issue campaigns, and we fully support this. Some prefer the kind of group that brings the positive satisfaction of helping some other women and themselves rather than taking on the monster of the nuclear establishment. Why campaign on an issue that is already the concern of a strong mixed movement – a movement in which women's role has been, and still sometimes is, making up the numbers and making the tea? Our answer is that feminism has an analysis of the whole of society, not just 'women's issues' like rape, abortion, women's health, and that it is important that feminists make clear and take action upon our analysis of issues like militarism and nuclear technology. If we can uncover the links between the arms race and male supremacy, a feminist society and a peaceful world will both be a little closer.

4
Organising a National Campaign: Women's Party for Survival, USA

SAYRE SHELDON

Taking the First Step

I believe that most people working for nuclear disarmament have had a form of 'conversion' experience – a specific realisation that nuclear weapons are real, and that they will be used if we continue to act like people picnicking on a railroad track with the train approaching.

My own came as I was driving to work one perfect May morning two years ago. I was enjoying the river and the trees when the scene abruptly vanished – blotted out, gone forever, no more springs with milky blue skies and pale new leaves – gone only for an instant but I could not forget it.

My realisation was less dramatic than that of another woman in our organisation: she happened to have her car radio on while driving her children home from school and heard a doctor describe the drugs that were being stock-piled in Washington to dispense after a nuclear attack, so that people could kill their suffering families. She saw herself lining up her children on the bed and giving them the pills. For a moment she *knew* how it would feel to kill her children, just as for a moment I *knew* that the natural world could disappear.

It's after an experience like this that one goes to work.

I had supported groups in the past that worked to end the arms race, with my cheques, phone calls, and letters to Washington. I knew a certain amount about SALT II and what the initials MIRV meant and that nothing so far had stopped more nuclear weapons from being built. Now the 'fire wall' between that knowledge and everyday life was gone and I had to begin really working.

Like many people, I chose the Women's Party for Survival because of Dr Helen Caldicott rather than anything I knew about the party. I had been hearing about a remarkable woman from Australia who had given up her medical research to go around the United States speaking about the effects of radiation on human beings. Eventually I saw the film, *Eight Minutes to Midnight*, a documentary about Dr Caldicott's life, and a few weeks later was invited to meet her. Arriving late, I rang the bell and Dr Caldicott opened the door. I followed her around until she wrote my name down; the next day a call came asking me to a meeting of the Women's Party National Council.

What explains Dr Caldicott's effect on people? They are in the the first place probably people who have had a 'conversion' experience, or at least have deep fears about nuclear war. They only need someone to convince them that something can be done about preventing it. So though her effect has been called charismatic, I don't see any mystery about it – she is simply able to transmit her feelings to others: her love for the miracle of human life, her anger at those who threaten it, her hope for the possibilities of preserving it. Looking rather small and alone on the platform, her strong voice and simple words are proof of the power one individual can have against enormous forces. Although she denies that she is a feminist and wants to enlist men and women in a single-issue campaign to get rid of nuclear weapons, she speaks to emotions our culture has labelled (and suppressed) as 'feminine' – the life-affirming side of us which must overcome the destructive side if we are to pull back from the brink.

I had only been to one meeting of the Council when I got a last-minute call to go to a week-end peace conference, and found myself describing the Women's Party for Survival to several hundred women when I had very little idea myself of what it was. The brochure I was handing out didn't explain enough either. It was an experience typical of many to follow: I was unprepared, trying to fill a gap, learning by doing – like the whole mushrooming nuclear disarmament movement.

I learned that the Women's Party had been organised in the summer of 1980 by Dr Caldicott in response to the people, primarily women, who came up after hearing her speak to ask what they could do. She explained later that as an Australian, she hadn't understood that it was almost impossible for a women's peace party to make any progress within our two-party political system. But the policy of the Party when I joined in 1981 still included the intention of running candidates for office. Until the time I joined, the Party had been run from living-rooms; now it had an office, donated for a year: four smallish rooms already crowded with boxes of publications, petitions and brochures; the walls covered with flyers and newspaper clippings; a veteran spider-plant struggling for survival in the front window; and a hot-plate producing many cups of coffee and tea. Two women served as co-directors without pay; a man, also unpaid, sent out publications and compiled the mailing-list; another woman, the only paid staff member, answered the phone, opened the mail, interviewed and directed the volunteers. The office was instantly familiar to me, because I had worked for other causes over the years: political campaigns for progressive candidates, anti-Vietnam projects. I recognised the intensity, dedication and spirit of cooperation along with the disorganisation, duplication, and lack of funds. A young, hopeful, and growing organisation – only this time, the task was much larger, the goals more long-range.

The National Council met in the acting-president's living-room: fifteen women, mostly young, many with small children. At the first meeting I went to, Dr Caldicott appeared, made a series of brisk comments about what needed to be done for the Mother's Day rally in Washington, and left early to prepare for a cross-country lecture tour beginning the next day. The strengths and weaknesses of the Women's Party were obvious from this meeting: we were a national organisation founded by one woman who went round the country sowing her message like a nuclear Johnny Appleseed, while here in Cambridge, a handful of women were responsible for setting up a programme to make effective activists out of all these converts.

As I saw it, the Council was strong in energy, creativity, and commitment; less strong in experience, recognition and funds. It operated with a refreshing lack of hierarchy and protocol, opinions and feelings were freely expressed, and its function was clearly not one only of organising, but also of coping with the emotional strains of working on this issue. The rapid and tumultuous growth of opposition to nuclear weapons was now threatening to make this informal structure inadequate.

Larger Steps

The summer of 1981 came and went with its characteristic interruptions: vacations, hot weather, children home from school. Some of us met each week at the office for a course in public speaking, practising our five-minute speeches on 'psychic numbing' and other topics on each other. The experience was valuable, but by fall the projected Speakers' Bureau had not materialised, and there were other signs that a consistent direction for the Party had not emerged. Dr Caldicott was spending most of her time with the older organisation of which she had become president, *Physicians for Social Responsibility*, whose mission it was to awaken the American public to the 'final epidemic' nature of nuclear war, and which was already achieving great success. The physicians' work only made ours more essential; once aroused to the dangers, people had to be given something to do. But meanwhile a whole series of new groups were forming and our need to establish a firm purpose and identity was becoming more urgent.

By fall the political climate had changed. The Reagan administration was revealing itself: President Reagan's statement about the possibility of a limited nuclear war in Europe, Secretary of State Haig's reference to a 'warning-shot,' and other efforts by government and Pentagon officials to make nuclear war 'thinkable' had done more than coalesce sentiment against nuclear weapons abroad, they had back-fired at home. Reagan's administration was also creating an increasingly regressive climate for women: conservatives pushed for women's return to home and family, day-care and other programmes for working-women were cut back, the anti-abortion movement gained new force, and it began to look as if the Equal Rights Amendment would certainly be defeated. As a result,. women were beginning to defect from their traditional political allegiances, realising that a system which cared so little about them could hardly be trusted with the future of their children or their country.

Over the next few months things changed even more rapidly. The economy was getting worse, the huge military budget was under attack, cities and towns were acting to adopt nuclear freeze referendums. My own city of Cambridge had been first in the country to take federal funds allocated to civil defence and use them instead for a booklet showing that the only defence is prevention. New possibilities for nuclear disarmament action were appearing daily in the newspapers, groups were forming, and Boston, traditionally a centre for progressive movements, was where many of these groups began: doctors, lawyers, teachers, musicians, the list kept lengthening. Older organisations, including some of the women's groups who had worked for peace in the past, were reemerging with new impetus and direction.

Reorganisation
The Women's Party meanwhile was being afflicted with severe growing pains. One of the co-directors was felt not to be delegating enough, and her own political ambitions to be taking precedence

over the Party's growth. The more feminist members wanted to include other issues besides disarmament. The office did not have the capacity to seek new members or keep in touch adequately with those we had. At the same time, the number of chapters had grown to fifty, valuable work was being initiated in many parts of the country, and there was no doubt that the Women's Party had a future.

After a painful interlude in which the co-director in question was asked to take leave of absence and refused, holding up all the Party's operations, we formed a new board. We also hired a consultant with much experience in both disarmament issues and setting up organisations, had a series of long gruelling meetings and emerged with a new name, a stronger identity, a clearer set of goals, and the renewed support of Dr Caldicott, who for a time had been too busy and too unsure of our direction to give us much help.

It is important for other groups to know that this kind of experience can be expected, worked through, and in the end, can produce a strengthened organisation. There were damages of course: the loss of time which could otherwise have been devoted to our programme, the confusion which discouraged some of our members, the loss of valuable people who had been with the Party since it began. Organisations run by women may avoid some of the mistakes and rigidities of traditional patriarchal ones, but they will inevitably encounter other problems. I learned that competitive-ness, anger, inability to communicate, and other human failings will surface in working for peace just like anywhere else.

Like the Party, I was learning many things – often after the initial mistake had been made. Like most of the women I worked with, I was finding the days too short for family and friends, jobs, and disarmament work at the same time. My book got put aside, but my teaching resumed, demanding its usual amount of time and energy. All of us made compromises as well as many hasty decisions; all of us believed that the situation was (and is) an emergency – the arms race had to be slowed down before a new and yet more dangerous 'generation' of weapons could be built. In December I agreed to be president of our board, and now to my day-time work could add the night-time worries about where our money was going to come from or whether a policy decision had been the right one.

A good example of a major worry was our name change – an account of this does much to explain how we see ourselves and what we hope to become. From the start, Dr Caldicott's idea for the party was that it should be open to everyone and that it should have only one goal – the control and eventual abolition of nuclear weapons.

She did not see this issue as a feminist one, and with some difficulty and dissension, other feminist-related issues were kept out. If the Women's Party had identified itself with the women's movement, it would have lost its chance to become broadly-based and to appeal to the vast majority of women in this country who still hold traditional views on women's roles. Dr Caldicott's intuition was correct: the feeling that motivated most women who had taken up this issue was neither feminist nor political – it was at the most basic level. Life on earth was being threatened and people were beginning to understand this. Like anything organic, this genuinely grass-roots movement would have a dynamic of its own; those of us working in it would have to grow and adapt with it.

The name had caused confusion from the beginning. It gave no clear indication of what we were; it raised the question of what we could accomplish as a political party in a traditional two-party system: the word 'survival' was being used by people who were actually preparing for nuclear war by building shelters; and while firmly committed to remaining an organisation run by women the word 'woman' in the title was making it difficult to organise in the more conservative areas of the United States where we felt our work was most needed. Letters from our members asked for a clearer name: requests for a change came from many of our chapter heads. Our consultant pointed out our need to seek tax-deductible contributions, which as a political party we could not raise. The voices in favour of change won out.

The Women's Party became two 'sister' organisations: one educational and therefore tax-deductible; the other political and supported by dues from its members. This is a common procedure in the United States, but there is nothing simple about it: countless forms had to be completed and filed, articles of incorporation and bye-laws had to be revised and rewritten, many trips to state offices had to be made. For a while I wondered if we had not become so mired in bureaucracy that we were becoming part of the problem rather than the solution. But by February of 1982 the transformation was completed: the old Women's Party had been renamed Women's Action for Nuclear Disarmament – our political arm – and a new organisation, Action for Nuclear Disarmament Education Fund, had been created.

We kept 'women' in the name of our political branch because the goal of getting more women to be politically active in nuclear disarmament was our major one. (The acronym WAND suggested auspicious results!)

The chapters were all notified of the changes, told that they were now an affiliate of WAND, and advised to choose whatever name seemed most appropriate, including keeping the old one if they preferred it. This looser structure encouraged autonomy and local initiative, but to help groups organise and new groups to form, we had a rewritten and expanded *Organising Manual* available from the national office (see Resources).

The education fund (AND) meanwhile, under its separate board, drafted a target budget, received a few large donations to get started, and began to prepare proposals for foundation grants. The budget described the minimum needed for running the office, sending out mailings, and hiring a staff: an administrative director, a special projects consultant, a mailing specialist, and an office manager were considered essential, although only the latter was listed as a full-time job or could be paid in full. (We all know that the person who runs the office is the key to efficiency and continuity in a largely volunteer organisation – the rule is to beg, borrow or steal to get a good one.) All employees can be paid as consultants at first to avoid witholding taxes and the myriad forms these entail. The goal was to have all staff on regular salary with full benefits but four months later we were only partly there. Other items in the budget were for as yet unrealised goals: a copying-machine, a computer, a WATTS telephone line (for unlimited long-distance calls).

The office, even without electronic assistance, was running more smoothly, work on a resource library and publications list had begun, a volunteer schedule was being set up – the new organisation was launched.

An Avalanche of Mail
The pieces were scarcely in place when AND was struck by a deluge. A smart and concerned Hollywood agent had arranged for Dr Caldicott to speak on one of the nation's most popular TV talk-shows along with two movie stars. After Dr Caldicott gave her horrifying picture of what a single bomb could do to one city, one of the stars turned to her and said, 'But, Helen, what can we do?' and Helen's answer was, 'You can write to Action for Nuclear Disarmament in Watertown, Massachusetts.' (Had we been still only a political organisation, our name could not have been mentioned on TV – except in a paid political advertisement.) A few days later, a truck drove up to our office and delivered four boxes of mail.

People of all ages and backgrounds wrote. Their letters were asking for help – help with a fear with which they had till now felt alone, the fear of annihilation. Volunteers read the letters in the office or took bundles of them home. Reading them was a powerful experience; people often cried. Each letter was answered with a form letter and an article by Dr Caldicott, a list of resources for learning more about the issue, and a sheet showing the locations of the affiliated groups. Those letters that were classified as 'poured their heart out' also received a personal note from the volunteer. Many who wrote sent in small contributions, often a dollar bill pinned to their letter. All names were put on the AND mailing list and would later get the AND newsletter; if they had shown interest in doing political work, they also were sent a WAND bulletin.

If people also expressed interest in starting a local group, they were helped with suggestions and encouraged to buy our *Organising Manual*. Every week, many requests come in for this manual, and the number of affiliated groups had by early 1982 reached seventy. In my home area, for example, there was a Cambridge Action for Nuclear Disarmament, a Newton Action for Nuclear Disarmament, and several more – each with its own elected officers and bye-laws, newsletter, and programme of events and fund-raising activities. Each group has a definite character. When we met with some of the representatives of groups from around the country in New York for the UN demonstration, we were struck by these differences. Some large California groups had kept the original Women's Party name and were continuing to find a strong feminist emphasis effective in their work; in more conservative areas, the groups described using moderate tactics to gain acceptance: a study-group in the library or Parent-Teachers Association, for example. Each affiliated group pays WAND a small yearly fee in return for the materials, advice and coordinating help they get from the national office. Increasingly these groups will be integrated into a network capable of responding to legislative alerts and doing sustained congressional lobbying for elections.

Others who write or call the national office do not want to start or join an affiliate group, but choose to be sponsors of AND, receiving, for a small contribution, our newsletter, resource lists (from which publications, films, etc, can be ordered), updates on important issues, and other mailings. Sponsors are encouraged to make tax-exempt gifts to enable AND to broaden its outreach and educational activities. Others will go to work for other disarmament groups: AND expects people to work where they feel most comfortable and effective. A teacher, for example, may decide to join the recently formed Educators for Social Responsibility and begin to work with the issues and fears of nuclear war in the classroom. A housewife may decide to work with her local club, alerting its members to the dangers of nuclear war and encouraging them to take action.

Another person may decide that a nuclear freeze is the main issue and work for the National Freeze Committee, which collaborates closely with our organisation. The important thing is to get people into active programmes so that their initial response does not subside into passivity and powerlessness.

With Dr Caldicott as a catalyst, we have a tremendous grass-roots potential; with her help (she is a member of both boards and keeps closely in touch) we expect to keep enlarging our scope and at the same time working more with other groups. Dr Caldicott learns from working with us as well: reformers tend to be loners, but she has to hear our concerns and problems. When for instance some of us met her to discuss a prospective Mother's Day rally on Boston Common, it was clear that Dr Caldicott hoped for a big, European-style demonstration; but we were able to convince her of the value a smaller, more family-oriented event would have. When the rally was nationally televised for just those qualities, all of us were pleased with the outcome.

Another major strength is in our volunteers: the national office has over eighty – some working regularly enough to be counted as staff, others coming in when they can and often taking work home. This is the place to add that some of our most hard-working volunteers (and staff and board members) are men. One, who works daily on our mailing list, has given up a lucrative computer-programming job to do so. A lawyer on our board, and an accountant who is a consultant, donate a great deal of professional service. And then there are the countless supportive husbands who put up with the absence of wives, stay at home with the children, or show up at rallies, lugging boxes and setting up the tables. As many as a third of our letters come from men: they write just as passionately about their fears for their children and the future as the women. As yet, I don't have information about how many men have actually joined: we have a family membership as well as a single one, but we will certainly remain a largely female organisation and our policy is to have a majority of women in leadership roles. There is still much to do to make women more active politically, but it is becoming clear that this growing citizens' revolt agains military thinking is transforming the old male–female dichotomies, so that perhaps some day we shall be able to talk of 'People's Action for Nuclear Disarmament.'

In the four months that followed the first avalanche of mail, there were several more as Dr Caldicott repeated this show and did others. More than 20,000 letters came in, from all parts of the country, including those we had thought inaccessible to us because they were too conservative. In the hectic process of responding, AND has corrected many of its first mistakes, improved its publications, and learned some hard lessons about the cost of large mailings. New needs have become clear: for more staff, more space, more efficient systems for using a mailing-list of over 25,000 names. So far we have received only two small grants and have depended on small personal contributions, and larger ones from our own fund-raising events and solicitations. Larger grants will have to be obtained if we are to make the necessary changes – and they are not easy to get.

How long will the present feeling of urgency about nuclear disarmament last? If President Reagan convinces the public that his efforts at negotiating are sincere, will their fears subside? For AND and WAND, the answer is only to go ahead, educate people about *real* arms control, assume that the money will come in, continue working as hard as we are now, and expect the struggle to be a long one.

Looking Ahead
We recognise that demonstrations are only one part of a nuclear disarmament campaign, and that education and political organising are of equal if not greater importance. So our programmes include: continuing to educate our members and others in the realities of the US and Soviet nuclear capabilities; keeping up the pressure for a nuclear freeze; encouraging local resistance to federal Civil Defence planning; and, most importantly, developing a system of legislative alerts and Congressional district lobbying for elections.

On 13 June 1982, the day after the largest demonstration against nuclear weapons (750,000) ever held in this country, WAND held a workshop on congressional lobbying techniques for our members from different parts of the country at the United Nations Plaza. I had marched the day before with my children and grandchild and was still feeling the euphoria of the experience. On the 13th, as I settled down with the fifty other people who had come to the workshop to learn about strategies for the months ahead, I sensed a different kind of power than that emanating from thousands of demonstrators. The few people in this room were going back to where they came from to teach others how, in Dr Caldicott's phrase, 'to use their democracy.' WAND had come of age.

5

All is Connectedness: Scenes from the Women's Pentagon Action, USA

YNESTRA KING*

(This is my own story of the WPA. It is not an attempt to represent the group. Each of us has her own story, and our collective story could only be written collectively.)

April 1979, Amherst, Massachusetts

I was a graduate student writing my comprehensive examinations in feminist theory, running between my life as a teacher and my life as a student, and squeezing in some political activity. I was trying to work out the thought behind the coming together of feminism and ecology, and my intuition that these are and should be connected. The nuclear power plant at Three-Mile Island Pennsylvania melted down as I completed the exam process, alternating between the typewriter and the television, listening to male technocrats talk about slamming rods into the core to stop the reaction, referring to the runaway nuke as a 'her' who needed to be 'cooled down'. I argued with my feminist friends about whether nukes (power and weapons) were really 'feminist issues'. I knew that it was time for me to become politically active again, as I imagined millions of women all over the planet 'taking the toys away from the boys'. I decided to begin talking seriously to other feminists in New England who shared my ecological perspective, about getting women together to talk about our fears for our own lives and the life of the Earth and what we could do together.

So, as with most good ideas whose time has come, I found out that

*with thanks to Eileen Kane for her support during the writing.

several other women were thinking the same thing. We were from different movements, feminist, lesbian, disarmament, anti-nuclear, ecology, and now after Three Mile Island we were ready to make a major commitment to bring our communities together to resist male violence against the living world. We decided to call a gathering so we could meet each other, share ideas and information, celebrate women's culture, and begin to develop an eco-feminist network and decentralised resistance/visionary movement. We wanted to resist all forms of domination, but we were especially concerned with connecting misogyny and the domination of women to the hatred of nature and drive to dominate nature which had led to the near annihilation of Pennsylvania that spring.

Fall 1979, Northampton, Massachusetts

I plunged into a year of organising, learning, and personal trans-formation which led to the Conference on Women and Life on Earth: Eco-feminism in the Eighties, which was held in March of 1980. Over seven hundred women from all over the northeast came (we turned women away when we reached that number). Women talked movingly about many issues and the connections between them. All along in planning the conference we had brainstormed, about what kind of actions would embody vision and show our fear for life on earth. The Pentagon emerged as the symbol of all the male violence we opposed. It is the real workplace of the American generals who plan the annihilation of the world as their daily work, far removed from the lives they imperil and the murders they commit. We wanted it to be clear to women around the world that there is feminist awareness of, and opposition to, the imperialist role of the United States military over the globe.

So we talked to the women who came to the Conference on Women and Life on Earth about a women's action at the Pentagon. All summer women all over New England and in New York City talked to each other about going to the Pentagon. The idea had caught their imaginations and taken root. It was time to start planning.

11 September 1980, Hartford, Connecticut.

This was the first meeting of the Women's Pentagon Action. I knew when I began looking forward to all-day meetings that something extra-ordinary was happening. I don't knit, I'm not very patient, and I'm often the first one to say 'let's vote' while other women are

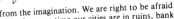

These are the frightening facts and the hopeful id

We invite you to read them

We are gathering at the Pentagon on November 16 because we fear for our lives. We fear for the life of this planet, our Earth, and the life of the children who are our human future.

We are women who come in most part from the northeastern region of our United States. We are city women who know the wreckage and fear of city streets, we are country women who grieve the loss of the small farm and have lived on the poisoned earth. We are young and older, we are married, single, lesbian. We live in different kinds of households, in groups, families, alone; some are single parents.

We work at a variety of jobs. We are students-teachers-factory workers-office workers-lawyers-farmers-doctors-builders-waitresses-weavers-poets-engineers-homeworkers-electricians-artists-blacksmiths. We are all daughters and sisters.

We have come here to mourn and rage and defy the Pentagon because it is the workplace of the imperial power which threatens us all. Every day while we work, study, love, the colonels and generals who are planning our annihilation walk calmly in and out the doors of its five sides. They have accumulated over 30,000 nuclear bombs at the rate of three to six bombs every day.

They are determined to produce the billion-dollar MX missile. They are creating a technology called Stealth—the invisible, unperceivable arsenal. They have revived the cruel old killer, nerve gas. They have proclaimed Directive 59 which asks for "small nuclear wars, prolonged but limited." The Soviet Union works hard to keep up with United States initiatives. We can destroy each other's cities, towns, schools, children many times over. The United States has sent "advisors," money and arms to El Salvador and Guatamala to enable those juntas to massacre their own people.

The very same men, the same legislative committees that offer trillions of dollars to the Pentagon have brutally cut day care, children's lunches, battered women's shelters. The same men have concocted the Family Protection Act which will mandate the strictly patriarchal family and thrust federal authority into the lives we live in our own homes. They are preventing the passage of ERA's simple statement and supporting the Human Life Amendment which will deprive all women of choice and many women of life itself.

We are in the hands of men whose power and wealth have separated them from the reality of daily life and from the imagination. We are right to be afraid.

At the same time our cities are in ruins, bankrupt; they suffer the devastation of war. Hospitals are closed, our schools deprived of books and teachers. Our Black and Latino youth are without decent work. They will be forced, drafted to become the cannon fodder for the very power that oppresses them. Whatever help the poor received is cut or withdrawn to feed the Pentagon which needed about $500,000,000 a day for its murderous health. It extracted $157 billion dollars last year from our own tax money, $1800 from a family of four.

With this wealth our scientists have been corrupted; over 40% work in government and corporate laboratories that refine the methods for destroying or deforming life.

The lands of the Native American people have been turned to radioactive rubble in order to enlarge the nuclear warehouse. The uranium of South Africa necessary to the nuclear enterprise, enriches the white minority and encourages the vicious system of racist oppression and war.

The President has just decided to produce the neutron bomb, which kills people but leaves property (buildings like this one) intact.

There is fear among the people, and that fear, created by the industrial militarists is used as an excuse to accelerate the arms race. "We will protect you . . . " they say, buy we have never been so endangered, so close to the end of human time.

We women are gathering because life on the precipice is intolerable.

We want to know what anger in these men, what fear which can only be satisfied by destruction, what coldness of heart and ambition drives their days.

We want to know because we do not want the dominance which is exploitative and murderous in international relations, and so dangerous to women and children at home—we do not want that sickness transferred by the violent society through the father to the sons.

What is it that we women need for our ordinary lives, that we want for ourselves and also for our sisters in new nations and old colonies who suffer the white man's exploitation and too often the oppression of their own countrymen?

We want enough good food, decent housing, communities with clean air and water, good care for our children while we work. We want work that is useful to a sensible society. There is a modest technology to minimize drudgery and restore joy to labor. We are determined to use skills and knowledge from which we have been excluded—like plumbing or engineering.

ysics or composing. We intend to form women's
s or unions that will demand safe workplaces,
f sexual harassment, equal pay for work of com-
le value. We respect the work women have done
ring for the young, their own and others, in
taining a physical and spiritual shelter against
reedy and militaristic society. In our old age we
ct our experience, our skills, to be honored
ised.

e want health care which respects and under-
ds our bodies. Physically challenged sisters must
 access to gatherings, actions, happy events,
k. For this, ramps must be added to stairs and we
t become readers, signers, supporting arms. So
e, so many, why have we allowed ourselves not to
w them?

/e want an education for children which tells the
 story of our women's lives, which describes the
h as our home to be cherished, to be fed as well
iarvested.

Ve want to be free from violence in our streets and
ur houses. One in every three of us will be raped in
ur lifetime. The pervasive social power of the mascu-
 ideal and the greed of the pornographer have
ne together to steal our freedom, so that whole
ghborhoods and the life of the evening and night
ve been taken from us. For too many women the
rk country road and the city alley have concealed
e rapist. We want the night returned, the light of the
oon, special in the cycle of our female lives, the stars
d the gaiety of the city streets.

We want the right to have or not to have children—
 do not want gangs of politicians and medical men
 say we must be sterilized for the country's good. We
now that this technique is the racists's method for
ontrolling populations. Nor do we want to be pre-
ented from having an abortion when we need one.
Ve think this freedom should be available to poor
omen as it always has been to the rich. We want to be
ree to love whomever we choose. We will live with
women or with men or we will live alone. We will not
llow the oppression of lesbians. One sex or one sex-
ial preference must not dominate another.

We do not want to be drafted into the army. We do
not want our young brothers drafted. We want *them*
equal with *us*.

We want to see the pathology of racism ended in
our time. It has been the imperial arrogance of white
male power that has separated us from the suffering
and wisdom of our sisters in Asia, Africa, South
America and in our own country.

Many North American women look down on the
minority nearest them: the Black, the Hispanic, the
Jew, the Native American, the Asian, the immigrant.

Racism has offered privilege and convenience; women often fail to see that they themselves have bent to
the unnatural authority and violence of men in government, at work, at home. Privilege does not increase
knowledge or spirit or understanding. There can be no
peace while one race dominates another, one people,
one nation, one sex despises another.

We must not forget that tens of thousands of
American women live much of their lives in cages,
away from family, lovers, all the growing-up years of
their children. Most of them were born at the intersec-
tion of oppressions: people of color, female, poor.
Women on the outside have been taught to fear those
sisters. We refuse that separation. We need each other's
knowledge and anger in our common struggle against
the builders of jails and bombs.

We want the uranium left in the earth and the earth
given back to the people who tilled it. We want a system of energy which is renewable, which does not take
resources out of the earth without returning them. We
want those systems to belong to the people and their
communities, not to the giant corporations which
invariably turn knowledge into weaponry. We want
the sham of Atoms for Peace ended, all nuclear plants
decommissioned and the construction of new plants
stopped. That is another war against the people and
the child to be born in fifty years.

We want an end to the arms race. No more bombs.
No more amazing inventions for death.

We understand all is connectedness. The earth
nourishes us as we with our bodies will eventually
feed it. Through us, our mothers connected the
human past to the human future. We know the
life and work of animals and plants in seeding, reseed-
ing and in fact simply inhabiting this planet. Their
exploitation and the organized destruction of never to
be seen again species threatens and sorrows us.

With that sense, that ecological right, we oppose
the financial connections between the Pentagon and
the multinational corporations and banks that the
Pentagon serves.

Those connections are made of gold and oil.

We are made of blood and bone, we are made of the
sweet and finite resource, water.

We will not allow these violent games to continue.
If we are here in our stubborn thousands today, we
will certainly return in the hundreds of thousands in
the months and years to come.

We know there is a healthy sensible loving way to live
and we intend to live that way in our neighborhoods
and our farms in these United States, and among our
sisters and brothers in all the countries of the world.

Unity Statement of the Women's Pentagon Action

still trying for consensus. When I arrived at the Quaker Meeting House in Hartford, women from many groups and places were assembled. There was plenty of grey hair, there were lots of mothers, and lots of lesbians. Everyone was sitting in a circle in kindergarten chairs getting acquainted and talking about whether feminism and a Washington action were antithetical, whether a women's action at the Pentagon would reinforce traditional images of women as caretakers, how to connect militarism and violence against women. None of us knew everyone at the meeting, there was no preset agenda, and the meeting was open to any women who wanted to come. But somehow, out of the group emerged a trust and a collective process which was to carry us through the action and into the formation of an ongoing Women's Pentagon Action. (Someone later suggested that sitting in very small chairs helped to keep anyone from feeling too self-important.)

We agreed that we were a group of concerned women acting as individuals. We were not a coalition of groups. We did not want some women to be more important in our group than others, and we didn't want the action to feature stars either. Somehow the Women's Pentagon Action had to reflect our feminist principles and process. And we began to talk about what these principles were. We talked about connections between violence against women and the rape of the earth. We talked about racism and American imperialism. We heard from women about the effect of military spending on the human services upon which women depend. We connected the masculinist mentality and nuclear bombs. Lesbian oppression and reproductive freedom were also issues that concerned us. We reflected on the election of Ronald Reagan and what that would mean to us. And we talked about how we might do our action with ritual politics and theatre and images and how many women we thought it would take to reach around the Pentagon. We were defining feminist resistance. Slowly the four stages of our action emerged – mourning, rage, empowerment, defiance.

We talked about what our Unity Statement should say, that it should say who we were, why we came together, and express our vision in a personal, non-rhetorical way. Grace Paley agreed to draft the statement, with input from anyone.

After the meeting a group of us went out to dinner and talked about feminist direct actions we had been part of. Shell from Hartford talked about an action she and a friend had taken against a pornography store which sold torture instruments, after they had leafletted and returned repeatedly to talk with the owner. They poured their own blood over the instruments and sat down. The police arrested them and kept them in jail for a week. After a long trial they were found not guilty. Another woman told of how a woman's affinity group in Vermont, known as the Spinsters, had woven shut the gates of a nuclear power plant with wool, string and rags as part of a civil disobedience action there. We sat for hours remembering all the times women have taken matters into our own hands and talking about what it was we would have to do again and again as we planned to go to the Pentagon.

September–October 1980, Northeast United States

The process of writing the Unity Statement as well as the politics it expresses set the way of working of the Women's Pentagon Action. For weeks Grace took phone calls, read the statement to women in her kitchen, on the subway, in New York, Vermont, Massachusetts. The spirit of unity from the Hartford meeting and the process of writing the statement and reaching consensus on it at our next planning meeting told our politics, and brought us together. We all listened to each other, everyone was heard and satisfied, and we took this statement home with us to organise.

16 and 17 November 1982, Washington DC

Two thousand women came to Washington for a day of workshops on Sunday, a vigil for black feminist Yolanda Ward, murdered the week before in Washington, and the Monday action. I was a press spokeswoman for the action. That meant I was supposed to explain what we were doing to the mostly male and very cynical press people who came to cover the action. It was 6.30 a.m. Monday as I persuaded the cab driver to let me stop for coffee on the way to the Dupont Circle Metro stop. That was all I was to have to eat in a day which ended at 2 a.m.

As we approached Dupont Circle I saw women with sleeping bags and backpacks approaching the escalator into the bowels of the Washington subway system. They were coming from all directions, and the sun was just coming up. I started getting excited and joined some other women. We stood out among the uniforms of bureaucrats and military personnel: I thought that some of these knew where we were going and had patronising smiles on their faces. I hoped we would have the last smiles that day. As we got off at Arlington I began to talk to reporters. Here we began the first stage of our action.

Mourning

We began our mourning by walking through the centuries of carnage at Arlington Cemetery, where the graves of war dead spread out as far as you can see. At Arlington even the tombstones stand at attention in neat military rows winding up and down the hills out of sight. It's an awesome scene.

I decided not to walk through Arlington and rode to the Pentagon with a reporter. When I got there, there were several sleepy, very bored TV crews in waiting. I noticed that the Pentagon is a very big building. The TV crews had also noticed that the Pentagon is a very big building, and they asked me sceptically whether we really thought we were going to reach all the way around. By then I had my own doubts but I said I was sure we would reach. At the entrance to Arlington 2000 women had looked like a lot of women but standing in the Pentagon parking lot alone with a bunch of cynical journalists I was worried. I guessed it would take at least 10,000 women to reach round and I knew we had only 2000. I was also worried that women wouldn't be able to mourn and rage on the spot – that it might feel phoney. All of us were the theatre, the actors, there were no speakers, no stage, no leaders – would this *work*?

The sounds of a drum beat and moans reached us before we saw the women. The NBC crew wandered to a corner of the building for a preview of the action as the women emerged from Arlington. One of them said 'Holy shit, will you look at that? What do you know!' as they sprinted for their cameras. Pentagoners crowded the windows to look. Guards began to slam and bolt doors and take up their positions to guard the entrances. Colourful puppets, banners and women in costume emerged from a tunnel leading from Arlington and walked rhythmically, slowly past the Mall Entrance to the River Entrance. The slow drumbeat and moans never let up as the black mourning puppet, twenty feet high, propelled along by women holding poles under her skirts, led this first stage of the action. We continued mourning as we made a circle. We stopped on a grassy lawn in front of the River Entrance and began to create our own cemetery, commemorating the women who have been victims of the war machines. We began by laying a gravestone commemorating the unknown woman.

I certainly didn't expect to cry. I didn't expect to scream. After all, I was an initiator of the action. I had been imagining women

Women gather round Ritual Mourning figure during the Women's Pentagon Action, 17 November 1980

Women plant tombstones outside the Pentagon, 17 November 1980

encircling the Pentagon for months. I knew exactly what was going to happen and I had the whole thing pretty well intellectualised. But as I watched the gravestones placed one by one – the unknown women, Karen Silkwood, Yolanda Ward, victims of illegal abortions, rape, war, racism, and as I stood observing other women mourning and interpreting the action for mostly male reporters, I felt as if I was being torn in two. So much for intellectualising. Finally I tore off the little card I was wearing that said 'Press'.

The rows of tombstones in our cemetery were in the foreground, and the rows of tombstones in Arlington stood out in the background. And if you turned around, the employees of the war department lined the steps and peered at us from windows as they took a small break from grim business as usual. We had no trouble weeping.

Rage
Then the drum tempo changed and the majestic rage puppet, in red, moved to the centre. The next stage of the action began and we raged and chanted 'We won't take it', 'No more war', 'Take the toys away from the boys'. Women railed at the Pentagon. And the crescendo built up. The people watching from the Pentagon looked astonished, some laughed, and some looked very uncomfortable.

By then I wasn't talking to the press at all. I was gripped in the experience and totally incapable of interpreting it to people outside of it. I was learning something about the power of ritual, the power of women together, and the depth of my own sorrow and rage.

I worry every day that they're going to kill everything. And I want to shake people on the streets and my friends and my family and sometimes I do. But having been raised on hellfire and brimstone Protestantism, I have an aversion to shaking people and screaming at them that they're going to die if they don't repent. I think constantly about how close we are to the end of the world. And I have believed for a long time that if any people are going to come up with a way of life and a way of doing politics which can save us, they will be women. Even so, I wasn't prepared for how I was transformed by that ritual. It felt as if something reached down inside me as I was playing my interpretive role, grabbed my tears and pulled them out of me. The feelings inside those other women touched the feelings in me and our rage built together. After a while the drumbeat changed and we began to move in two directions to start the encirclement. The yellow puppet moved to the front, signalling the next stage . . .

Empowerment

We were encircling the Pentagon, hand in hand, or holding scarfs and other women-extenders to help us reach around. The empowerment puppet went one way and the doves of peace and other puppets went the other. We sang songs of the women's movement, and songs of the civil rights movement. 'You Can't Just Take My Dreams Away' moved into 'We Shall Overcome', and 'We Shall Not Be Moved' gave way to 'Song of the Soul'. Runners raced around the Pentagon monitoring our progress around the building and relaying messages. By now Pentagon workers crowded the windows. A few women were seen giving us signs of solidarity from within the Pentagon. Later that day a woman coming out of the Pentagon told us that there was a lottery going on inside about whether we could reach all the way around. Odds were that we couldn't – how could a bunch of little women reach all the way round that great big building? Then came word that we were all the way around with women to spare. An enormous whoop filled the air and women waved clenched fists at the Pentagon. The final stage of our action began . . .

Defiance

At three entrances women moved up the steps, blocking the entrances with our bodies in non-violent civil disobedience. Mostly we sat down but at one entrance the Spinsters wove the doors shut, as they had at the nuclear power station in Vermont. Arrest policies were different at each entrance. At one, women were arrested immediately, at another there were few arrests all day, and at the River Entrance, where I was, arrests proceeded slowly and police lines held tight. Women talked with police and passers by all day, explaining and imploring.

The Pentagon police are almost all black. They mostly treated women gently and with respect. Some even confided sympathy with our action and explained that as black people (mostly men) living in Washington DC they had had a hard time getting jobs. Many of them are Vietnam veterans, conscripted to fight the Pentagon's wars. It was a confusing situation for us to encounter these black people between our mostly white demonstration and the white higher-ups at whom our opposition was directed.

I started up the left side of the steps at the River Entrance hand in hand with other women. I couldn't reach the door and I saw women arrested one by one. Some were carried up the steps and passed through the doors in front of me. As women were arrested they were taken inside the Pentagon. One woman yelled to a policeman carrying a woman inside, 'You be careful with her. She's precious to us'. In that moment we had a sense of our power, that each of us was precious to us all. I was standing in front of the police lines, watching the entrance as my turn came.

I heard a voice say, 'I want that one'. The police line opened up and two men dragged me inside and pushed me up against the wall to be searched. Even though I have been through non-violence training and being arrested and searched several times before, I was frightened by the manhandling and the search (done by a woman). As she held my hands to the wall, high over my head, and she felt me up and down, I remembered all the times I've been pushed, shoved or handled by men against my will because they were doctors, cops or lovers I was afraid to refuse. I could see familiar faces in the entrance through the blue uniforms around me. As they put the plastic hand cuffs on me and my friends said 'hello', I felt my heart slow down. The experience convinced me that women must have non-violence training in preparation for actions like this one. This training should include simulating arrest and search. Part of the training should also involve participants in talking about all the forms of violence we experience, and the personal and political connections between them.

Life in the Pentagon vestibule was lively. We had imaginary lines we weren't to step across, police contradicted each other and women crowded at the entrances to wave to us. We were taken downstairs six at a time to be booked. We were marched through the Pentagon in rows, down the escalator past the offices of the Joint Chiefs of Staff. Finally, we sat in rows in the basement garage. Some women were total non-cooperators – they refused to walk, talk or give their names. I walked and talked to whoever would listen. As we sat waiting to be booked we talked about non-cooperation and the politics of being arrested and jailed – we had very different ideas about how to proceed upon arrest, in court and in jail. We had our pictures taken with our arresting officers, and sat in buses for hours, waiting until the magistrates at the courthouse were ready for us.

Monday night

As we got to the courthouse we were arraigned slowly. Women who had decided to plead 'guilty', were sentenced. Women who had never before been arrested at the Pentagon got ten days, women who had been arrested before got thirty days. The courtroom scenes went on for hours. They were inspiring, poignant, funny, as woman after woman made moving speeches about military violence and violence against women, about how their fathers or husbands had beaten them, about walking the streets in fear, about being raped, about what we could do with all that money if it wasn't used for amazing inventions for death, and about why we had acted as women and as feminists. It was clear to me that even if the news reporters I had talked to earlier couldn't understand the connections we were trying to make, all the women taking part certainly did.

I pleaded 'not guilty'. I thought to myself, 'Let them prove that I blocked the entrance – I'm certainly not guilty of anything.' Women felt differently about the plea issue. I got out on twenty-five dollars bail (10% of my $250 bond) and I began trying to figure out how we could get other women out of jail. The sentences and the bond amounts were much stiffer than we had expected, and many of us were in the courthouse until 2 a.m., when the trials ended. The charge, blocking an entrance, is the equivalent of a parking ticket, for which people expect a small fine. No one was prepared to go to jail, or pay high bails. The sentences were extraordinary for the charge. They loaded convicted women on a bus headed for the federal prison in Alderson, West Virginia, twelve hours away. The

THE BIG DADDIES IN WASHINGTON ARE SAYING, "we know what's good for the nation..

keep the women barefoot and pregnan

push them back into the closet...

Take over the w
put Daddy over the f
A GUN and a chance

FOR THEIR GAMES...

and when they blow it up...
and all the people and animals
are burning and screaming...
and most are dead and dying
and the Big Daddies can't use
us anymore for anything...

keep the women & children quiet
~norant & praying...

terrify, sterilize & exterminate them ...

~nions, lower wages, raise prices,
~d reward men with a uniform,
and kill an enemy...

GIVE THE BIG BIG DADDIES
The world and all its goods...

oil, wheat, coal, bananas, gold,
land, water, air, atoms, genes, space
AND ALL THE $ THEY CAN TURN THESE INTO

WOMEN OF URANUS, HERE
COMES YOUR LOVER
AND SAVIOUR

Why, a few of
the BIGGEST
DADDIES will
come out of their
shelters and get on
their space shuttle and
go find another world to
kick around ....

NO

Sisters; let the patriarchs in Washington
hear from you! write, wire, organize
in your communities.

WOMEN'S PENTAGON ACTION
339 LAFAYETTE ST.   254 4961

please turn →

women were shackled together in leg irons and shackled at the waist.

30 November 1980, Northampton, Washington DC

My trial was 1 December. Four of us drove down and on the way stopped in New York City for a meeting, where we heard stories of Alderson from women who had served their ten days and been released. I was particularly struck by accounts of how many of the women federal prisoners are women of colour, how most are serving long sentences for 'conspiracy' (being associated with men who were convicted of crimes the women were presumed to have known about), how these women have no 'voice' on the outside, and of friendship among women in prison. We're learning that we can survive prison, and build wider bonds of solidarity between women. What important knowledge that is – that we can survive jail and be stronger and wiser for the experience! This was confirmed when the women who served thirty days at Alderson came back. Many women have continued active friendships with women they met in prison, and are now talking with other women about the prison experience and the political role of women's prisons.

At my trial I was found guilty. In pronouncing his verdict the judge (who'd been trying women for days) said that the state exists to protect people from each other, that violence is inherent in human nature, and that no people have ever lived in peace, all of which is untrue. Since I was going to jail anyway I decided to risk contempt of court and talk to the people in the courtroom about male rule, tribal people who've lived in peace, and the violent nature of the state. When I stopped talking the judge asked me if I had anything further to say and levied a $25.00 fine. I spent the rest of the day watching other women go to trial, making moving speeches and being sentenced to ten days. I left the courthouse glad to be free, but thinking about how my race, class, and privileged education (and pure luck) had enabled me to talk my way out of jail when other women who had acted with me were spending ten days (or more) locked up.

December 1980, St Augustine, Florida

By the middle of December I was exhausted, and ready for a vacation from politics. At the end of December I arrived at the Pagoda, a women's resort in Augustine, Florida, where I expected to escape politics and indulge in lesbian hedonism. As soon as I got there I knew that this visit would not be an escape, that what I would bring away was a knowledge of the impossibility of escape. My friends had barely said 'hello' when they began to tell me how two weeks before, as I had been going to trial for blocking an entrance to the Pentagon, thirty whales had beached themselves on the Pagoda beach, dying. Ten years ago the army dumped thousands of canisters of nerve gas 100 feet down in the Atlantic, ten miles off the Pagoda beach, and now the canisters are beginning to leak. I thought of the sunny days last spring when I collected shells, watched the porpoises and peacefully recovered from organising the Conference on Women and Life on Earth, far from the Pentagon, or so I had thought.

Women staying at the Pagoda were anxious to hear about the Women's Pentagon Action. My friend, Julie, told me that she and other women at the Pagoda who had not been politically active for years were now ready to be active again after years of building a separatist community where they thought they would be safe from male violence. That day she and several other women decided to start a group to meet with their neighbours along the beach to begin organising to do something about their own local Pentagon – the leaking gas canisters. The next day, as we were sunning ourselves after lunch, I heard a crash. A man rammed his car into the back fence. Crash again. A woman's voice 'Hey, what do you think you're doing?' A man's voice 'Take that you fucking lessies.' Nothing like this had ever happened before at the Pagoda. We spent the night with a croquet mallet and garden shears by the bed, as the wind whipped through the palm trees, the illusion of separation and safety dispelled.

How does one reconcile feminist anger with a philosophy of non-violence? Can I do this and at the same time sympathise with Joan Little, killing her jailer as he entered her cell to rape her? Or with the guerilla movements of El Salvador and South Africa? I have no absolute answers, but I am convinced that feminism and pacifism are integrally connected.

February to November 1981, Amherst, Massachusetts and the Pentagon

A hundred and fifty Women's Pentagon Action organisers met in February to evaluate the action. We decided to be an ongoing network and to return to the Pentagon for a second action in the fall. The second action was organised much like the first, but this time there was an information clearing house in Philadelphia, and an active local in Washington DC which handled logistics. As the sphere of the WPA activity extended southward to Washington DC, New York City became the mid-point and there was less participation by northern New England women in the second action. But we doubled our numbers, with women coming from all over the United States (and a few from Europe and South America). There were also actions inspired by ours in other parts of the US on the same day, and telegrams of support came from sisters in other places who couldn't be with us.

There were other changes between our first and second actions. In the first action, during our civil disobedience (defiance) stage most women sat down in front of the doors, linking arms. In the second action, defiance was more explicit and active, we first wove a braid around the Pentagon as we circled, and then wove all the entrances shut with yarn, moving back and forth past each other as Pentagon police moved back and forth cutting and tearing the yarn. We retied and started new weavings, with help from women who were not blocking entrances. There were cheers, chants, and whistles, and women sang as we wove. Generals minced their way through woman-made webs, amidst laughs and admonitions about their daily work. At the end there was a braid around the Pentagon, and beautiful weavings at all the entrances. Women who were not arrested held a closing ritual circle.

There were fewer women committing civil disobedience in the second action, partly because of the harsh sentences we knew to expect and partly because those of us who are committed to non-violent civil disobedience as a feminist tactic did not do enough explaining and educating. (Since the second action there have been many discussions of civil disobedience [c.d.] within the WPA.) Sixty five women took part in the c.d. Again, women were given ten- to thirty-day sentences. This time I did go to jail, as part of a bail solidarity action. ('Bail solidarity' means that everyone taking part in an action refuses to leave until everyone is released without having to pay bail – the argument is that bail discriminates against people without money.) I was imprisoned in a basketball court with over forty women for five days – those who had been sentenced were there for ten days. Those with sentences longer than ten days went back to Alderson (some women had fifteen- and thirty-day sentences).

Our statement from prison is printed on pages 58–60 below.

Web blocking the Pentagon entrance, 16 November 1981

Why We're Here
Statement from Arlington Jail, 19 November, 1981

We are 43 feminist women imprisoned in the Arlington, Virginia, county jail because for a while on Monday morning 16 November, 65 of us taking part in a demonstration of 3500 women blocked the entrances to the Pentagon. We were part of the 1981 Women's Pentagon Action where we mourned, raged and defied the chief architects of masculine violence in the place where they plan the annihilation of the world. Some of us threw blood on the pillars, symbolising the blood shed by women who are victims of male violence all over the world. Most of us wove the entrances shut with wool, string, rags, and for a time, we entangled the powers that would bury us. We are writing because we want you to know why we are here.

Some of us are serving ten day sentences, some of us are awaiting trial and doing bail solidarity, and some of us refused to be released on personal recognisance, and were consequently given a bail of $1000 each. We are a varied group: our ages are seventeen to sixty. Many of us are lesbians. We are from various class backgrounds. Some of us are physically challenged. We wish more women of colour could be here, but we recognise that the racism of the police, the courts, and the jails increases the risks taken in civil disobedience for women of colour.

We spend time talking, singing, playing basketball with a rolled-up jacket hood, meeting, making hats from newspaper, reading, writing, and wondering what's going to happen to us in court, and wondering what the principled response is to every level of confrontation with the authorities, from jailer, to Sheriff, to court, to state. It's hard living with forty-three women in a windowless basketball court, cots lining each wall and down the middle, wearing dirty clothes or prison clothes that don't fit; and meeting for hours daily to negotiate how we can live together without going mad from the crowding, noise and claustrophobia.

But we're also talking for hours every day about feminism and nonviolence, forms of resistance, and the various meanings and paths of noncooperation. Some of us are fasting, several of us refused to identify ourselves, and a few of us refused to walk ourselves. We are discovering that nonfreedom and even jail are a box within a box, and that resistance has many faces. But we choose to resist directly to build a feminist resistance movement, and most of us have found the experience of direct nonviolent confrontation to be tremendously empowering. 'Civil disobedience is addictive,' said one of us.

We've even had a sit-in here in jail: to keep the door of the bathroom open so we don't have to ask a jailer every time we want to use the bathroom or get a drink. A number of us sat in front of the door. As the Sheriff ordered a deputy to close it, the hall filled with deputies. A guard threatened us, telling us he could divide us up and send us to other jails and we'd be sorry, that he'd close the door if it took 100 US Marshalls to do it. But we sat still – singing 'You can't kill the spirit. She's like a mountain. Old and strong, she goes on and on. . .' And we sat still – defending our basic human dignity as prisoners, standing firm against one of the small humiliations which taken together make up the fabric of oppression. Finally they left and the door stayed open. A small victory perhaps, but prison is a series of small indignities and mind games designed to break a person's spirit and divide a group. We are resisting and learning about the system and about each other as we go along. We are learning a lot.

We came to this action as women and feminists, connecting crimes against us in our daily lives with the world-wide violence of the military machine. We came to resist the patriarchy because we fear for our lives and for the life of the planet at the hands of these power-hungry men. We want our sisters to understand why we see militarism as a feminist concern, and to understand how our action of nonviolent civil disobedience grew from our feminist vision and politics. We did not act to absolve men of responsibility for acting, or because we wish to capitulate to the traditional role of women forced to clean up after everyone else and to nurture men while denying ourselves. We acted because we fear for our own lives, and because we oppose the military mentality: that of rule by the biggest weapons, of penetration and domination, and of appropriation of our lives to keep this power structure intact. We see this military mentality as intimately tied to the oppression and fears we women live with every day – the fear of rape, the oppression of having our reproductive choices taken from us, the coercion of compulsory heterosexuality. This mentality works hand in glove with racism, using racism to justify imperialist aggression against Third World and native peoples in this country and abroad. These white men have stolen much from us and the theft is still going on.

We were arrested at the second Women's Pentagon Action. There, we used our bodies to disrupt what goes on in the Pentagon – if only for a brief time. We believe that direct action and massive nonviolent civil disobedience are absolutely necessary to stop the threat of nuclear annihilation. The everyday oppression of living in an increasingly authoritarian, militarised society is as much a feminist concern as reproductive rights or lesbian oppression. The Family Protection Act, which could also be called the Patriarchy Protection Act, attempts to force us into proper male-ruled nuclear families and to shape our consciousnesses so that we accept their authority. Our feminism is anti-authoritarian and anti-hierarchical. So we went to the Pentagon in an action which embodied our resistance to coercive authority in form and content. We planned and organised collectively, in a decentralised manner. We had no leaders or speeches. Our action consisted of four stages – first, we mourned all our sisters who have been victims of individual male violence or state violence by placing hundreds of tomb-stones commemorating these women. Then we raged, our anger fuelled by our mourning, and led by our red rage puppet. Then we empowered ourselves, encircling the Pentagon, led in two directions by our yellow and white puppets, to the beat of our drums. We wove a web around the Pentagon. As the defiance stage began, signalled by our black puppet, some of us blocked entrances. Sixty-five sisters were arrested. Forty-three of us

59

are in jail now, and others who have not yet gone to trial may go to jail in the future.

We want to see all these issues discussed widely in our movement – militarism, resistance, direct action, nonviolence, jail, and so on. Many of us aren't yet clear about the many dimensions, but we believe that it is essential that we resist, directly. And we believe that feminist women acting together have a special possibility of seeing what's wrong and of developing the forms of nonhierarchical cooperative direct action and civil disobedience which might help save our planet and usher in a free feminist future.

That's why they put us here.

Between the first and second actions we also talked a lot about racism. In our first action the mourning puppet was black. In the second action our black puppet led the empowerment phase. Both years it has been mostly white women who have participated in the action, and I don't think outreach has been sufficient either year. The second action featured a Sunday walk from our gathering place through a black neighbourhood to the Air and Space Museum, which features replicas of the bombs dropped on Hiroshima and Nagasaki. I am not sure what the black people who watched the spectacle thought about our parading through their neighbourhood with little communication beforehand on the purpose of our action, and no practical way to talk with people as we paraded through. Our anti-racist 'connection' is not as strong as it must become.

We need to make all the other connections stronger, between all the forms of domination we oppose, and to continue to evolve our aesthetic, participatory mode of action. We also need to work on our internal process of consensus decision-making.

Feminist process, including consensus, is difficult in an open continuing organisation such as the WPA. Consensus decision-making means that every decision must be agreeable to the whole group. The assumption behind consensus is that a collective decision is most desirable, and that one person may possess some piece of truth that others have overlooked. Any woman can block a decision. Most of the time, when women disagree with a decision they don't stand in the way of the group (they 'stand aside').

The spirit of the consensus process extends to written statements or leaflets of the group. It's quite an experience to write for the WPA, because everyone must be heard and satisfied. It's sometimes frustrating, but, mostly, what we come up with is better in the end than it would have been had one person been left on her own to write it. We avoid rhetoric, slogans, 'isms', party lines where possible – but when we say 'patriarchy' we mean all the inter-connected forms of domination and violence that we oppose. For example, our flyer which was to advertise our forum for International Women's Week on 'The Politics of Connectedness' was edged with the words PATRIARCHY RACISM PATRIARCHY SEXISM PATRIARCHY LESBIAN OPPRESSION PARTRIARCHY ECOLOGICAL DEVASTATIONetc.

Our participatory and aesthetic actions are still evolving, and we see their influence on the actions of other feminist and non-feminist groups. When we do actions we attempt to be true to all our connections. This is hard when we generate actions of our own, but even more difficult when we take part in actions sponsored by coalitions which are concerned with single issues. Our multi-issue commitment compels us to respond to outside pressures and join with other groups, but we have sometimes found ourselves feeling pulled in too many directions and fragmented. I am now part of the New York local, which has been involved in actions around Haitian refugees, El Salvadorean violence against women, the eviction of the lesbian health clinic, and other pressing issues.

Our deeply woman-identified politics mean that the WPA is made up of women who love and identify with women, many of whom are lesbians. There are a number of women who attribute their becoming aware of lesbianism as a choice, and their subsequent coming out as lesbians, to their work with the WPA. There are struggles, strains and continuing discussions about homophobia, and how to have a stronger lesbian visibility in a mixed group. But the NY WPA – lesbian, straight, bisexual, undecided, etc. – marched with our banner in the NY Gay Pride march last year. Other locals have done similar actions in their communities.

One action was to organise a feminist presence at the 12 June 1982 demonstration for disarmament, which coincided with the United Nations Special Session on Disarmament in New York City. Women walked beneath an eight-foot globe (a helium weather balloon) which floated high in the air. A giant banner beneath the balloon carried the theme of our walk, 'A feminist world is a nuclear-free zone'. Individual walkers carried streamers which told about a feminist world: treasuring the earth, reproductive choice, sexual freedom, healthy food, diversity; and announced that in a feminist world there would be no bosses, no hunger, no rape, no lesbian oppression, no beauty contests, no boredom! Many of us joined in women's affinity groups to blockade the missions of the nuclear powers in a civil disobedience action on 14 June. Some of us did Tai Chi in unison, mesmerising police and getting around barricades; others of us wore bibs that said 'Disarm the Patriarchy', and 'War is Man-Made', so that our connections would be visible to everyone watching the action.

WPA locals continue to function autonomously, taking actions against their own local Pentagons. The locals tend to function as affinity groups of the whole, attempting to embody the integration

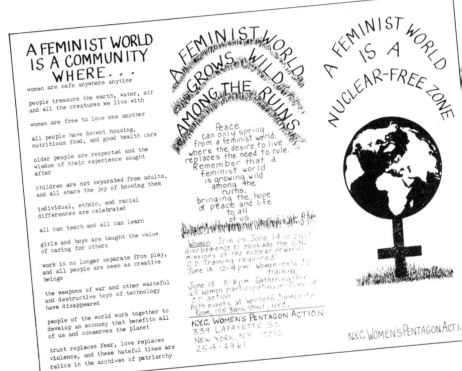

A FEMINIST WORLD IS A COMMUNITY WHERE...

women are safe anywhere anytime

people treasure the earth, water, air and all the creatures we live with

women are free to love one another

all people have decent housing, nutritious food, and good health care

older people are respected and the wisdom of their experience sought after

children are not separated from adults, and all share the joy of knowing them

individual, ethnic, and racial differences are celebrated

all can teach and all can learn

girls and boys are taught the value of caring for others

work is no longer separate from play, and all people are seen as creative beings

the weapons of war and other wasteful and destructive toys of technology have disappeared

people of the world work together to develop an economy that benefits all of us and conserves the planet

trust replaces fear, love replaces violence, and these hateful times are relics in the archives of patriarchy

A FEMINIST WORLD GROWS WILD AMONG THE RUINS

Peace can only spring from a feminist world, where the desire to live replaces the need to rule. Remember that a feminist world is growing wild among the ruins, bringing the hope of peace and life to all of us.

Women: Join us June 14 in civil disobedience to blockade the U.N. missions of the nuclear powers. C.r. Training required. June 13 12–4 p.m. Women-only training.

June 13 5–8 p.m. Gathering for all women participating in June 14 c.r action. Both events at Westbeth Community Room, 155 Bank Street, NYC.

N.Y.C. WOMEN'S PENTAGON ACTION 339 LAFAYETTE ST. NEW YORK, NY 10012 254-4961

N.Y.C. WOMEN'S PENTAGON ACT.

A FEMINIST WORLD IS A NUCLEAR-FREE ZONE

of the personal and the political characteristic of the consciousness-raising groups of the seventies. I see it that way, that the c.r. groups in which most of us began to make the feminist connections, to see that the personal is political, need to become affinity groups, committed to taking political action as well as providing personal support. It is a natural evolution for feminism, and a necessary one. Those of us who are active in WPA locals see each other socially, and are close in different ways, much like sisters in consciousness-raising groups.

At the moment the Women's Pentagon Action speaks to (and from) the feminist movement, the peace movement, and the ecology movement. We say to everyone who will listen that there will be no peace without feminism, for in this world, war is man-made. And there is only one place, this one living Earth, where we can make our feminist world.

6

Babies Against the Bomb

A Statement by TAMAR SWADE

Being pregnant and in the anti-nuclear movement happened at the same time for me. I joined a study group with five other women and we gave talks on nuclear power. This led to our writing the booklet, *Nuclear Resisters*.

By then my baby had been born and the effort of demand-feeding it at the same time as researching and writing my share of the booklet was enormous. The group was wonderfully supportive, but I felt that the pressures of coping with a newborn baby – the lack of sleep, exhaustion and lack of time – clashed with the needs of an ordinary group. I wasn't free to run off and collect things or proof-read as the others were, and I could no longer get out easily in the evenings when the usual anti-nuclear/peace meetings take place.

I'd suddenly become a different kind of social being and I realised I needed to start a group where everybody understood my position because they were in it too, where it was fine to go 'brrm-brrm' or 'whoopsy!' to a child in the middle of a sentence if necessary, or change a nappy.

I found I'd joined a separate species of two-legged, four-wheeled creatures who carry their young in push-chair pouches, who emerge from their homes during the day to swarm the parks, forage in the super-markets and disappear without trace at nightfall. Occasionally some converged for a 'coffee morning' or a mother-and-baby group run by the National Childbirth Trust. Here there was much discussion about nappy rash, (not) sleeping and other problems pertaining to the day-to-day survival of mother and infant.

If only these thousands of women could inform and organise themselves, what an untapped force for peace! Why not start a mother-and-baby group whose discussions included *long-term* survival?

At first, therefore, we were called 'Mother and baby anti-nuclear group'. As this was rather a mouthful, we were somehow gradually shortened to 'Babies against the Bomb', which stayed with us. We meet during the day, with our babies or young children. Meetings are friendly and informal and we campaign wherever and however we feel we can be most effective.

Several women who have enquired about the group have never been involved in any campaigning at all, but the fact of having a child has made them think differently about the future. Those of us who had been involved before often feel an added urgency to our desire for peace after having a child.

There are some feminists who frown upon this attitude and I would like to answer them.

There is something utterly vulnerable and loveable about a new-born baby, something wholly fascinating about this creature whose every impulse is towards survival but who is so dependent for it upon others. Its cries wrench at one and it is agonising to think of someone so little and blameless being hurt.

I am responsible for its existence – and no amount of word-juggling can get away from this. It is my responsibility and my urgent desire to ensure its survival, to speak for its rights since it can't do so for itself.

And it's not only for my child I feel thus. The same feeling now extends to all children. Through my child the immorality of this world where people needlessly starve to death, has become intolerable. With pain I could not have known before, I grieve for those women in the Third World who hear their children crying for food but who can't feed them or themselves.

I know hundreds of women who feel this. Each of them in turn probably knows hundreds of others who feel the same. Some are feminists through and through, others don't know what 'feminism' means. One woman told me that the mention of nuclear war conjures up the waking nightmare of her children burning. Another

pictures kissing her children goodbye for the last time. A third said her particular nightmare was that the four-minute warning would come while she was at work and she wouldn't be able to cross town in time to get to them . . .

In fact, it seems that millions of women in numerous cultures throughout history have had similar experiences in relation to their children. Should we all feel ashamed of this deep gut-feeling? For me, feminism is about choice, about every woman's freedom to feel and act and be valued. Does it make me any less of a person if my immediate, instinctive reaction to nuclear war is in my capacity as a mother? Judging by my friends in the campaign who are mothers, certainly not! Does it mean that I suddenly care less about living myself? Rubbish! It's more that another dimension had been added to my caring.

Our priority is peace. What does it matter how we come to want it? Let's be tolerant, supportive, sisterly. This will make us stronger and more effective; we are less likely to succeed if we are divided. If *we* can't do it, what hope is there for the rest of the world?

7
Children Need Smiles not Missiles: Planning a Walk – Oxford Mothers for Nuclear Disarmament

JINI LAVELLE

The last two months of writing have been so painful that I hardly know why I have done it. In fact, my eyes well with tears when I think about it. For someone with greater self-confidence or more practical experience this must seem absurd, but writing is not my profession – I am an artist by training. Apart from the occasional hastily-scribbled adolescent poem, short story or essay, or increasingly infrequent entries in my journal, I write nothing but letters to friends. It has been like giving birth – exciting, immensely satisfying and excruciatingly painful – even an article as apparently simple as this. I'd rather wash dishes than reveal myself on paper. If you say something, it is soon forgotten; if you write it down, there is a permanence in the words, often ill-deserved and unintended. I've been doing a lot of dish-washing recently!

Much of the way we lead our life is a reaction to, or a rejection of our background and upbringing. In our Peace Group, three mothers are from pacifist backgrounds and four from military families, including myself. I was brought up a Roman Catholic and educated in a Convent boarding school, where I used to pray in front of the statues *not* to get a vocation (I now see some of the advantages in such a calling). I went to Oxford to study fine art, and then taught art and drama. Later I married an unconventional Irishman, as opposed to the intended English, preferably titled, public schoolboy. He is now a solicitor and we have three young sons, two of whom are successfully trying to distract me as I write this. And so I now appear to be a conventional middle-class housewife. I do not paint any more (you need to be strong, selfish and preferably have a wife – no wonder there are so few famous women painters!). My creative energies for the present go into my family and my home, my friends and the peace movement.

Until about two years ago, I had given little thought to the horrors of nuclear war, but the increasing press coverage and my growing friendship with Judith led me to a lecture on the effects of the bomb and a video recording of an Open University lecture given by Michael Pentz. I was horrified and outraged, and remain to this day passionately convinced of the immorality of nuclear warfare and weapons. I say this not as a pacifist but as a human being. What kind of society can support its leaders and rulers in the contemplation of the mass extermination of its own or another's population?

I joined the local anti-nuclear organisation and found myself with some strange bedfellows, uncomfortable with many of its politically extreme members and increasingly disillusioned with the in-fighting and arguments. Party politics seem irrelevant when successive governments of the right and left have pursued a nuclear policy since the Second World War. I am still a member.

The mothers' walk gave me an opportunity to take positive action, working with mothers with whom I feel comfortable, accepted and uncriticised. I have become deeply fond of these women. I speak later of the group and how it worked. Helping to organise the mothers' walk and all the other activities and events we have been involved in since, has contributed to a greater self-awareness – to know for example, that I am a feminist. Its meaning is difficult to define (we are not a feminist group) but for me being a woman and a feminist are inseparable. And I've gained a greater self-confidence, enough to attempt to put my thoughts down on paper. I had always felt that a record should be made for the benefit of other mothers and women wishing to do the same. I dislike labels and as I am not a wholefood, hairy men and haversack addict, I wanted to show that women like myself also have something to contribute to the peace movement. In fact, sometimes I feel like turning up at rallies in a garden party outfit, but that is just the actress manquée in me!

The idea for a mothers' walk for Nuclear Disarmament was Judith's. She had suggested it at a meeting of Campaign Atom, Oxford's local nuclear disarmament group. Through personal contacts, playgroups and school a meeting was arranged at Julia's house in April 1981 of women with sympathetic views. There were eleven mothers at that first meeting, where Judith outlined her idea for a peaceful mothers' and childrens' protest as the escalation of the nuclear arms race – a walk through the centre of Oxford, ending in a park, with picnics and entertainment for the children.

We felt this number was large enough to form a workable 'committee', where decisions could be taken by all of us. In what became a hallmark of the group, no leaders asserted themselves that night, no budding committee members emerged to organise the group, but two 'chairwomen' were somehow found despite themselves to coordinate the work and provide an agenda for our meetings. This plan became a source of consternation and hilarity as week by week the mythical agenda never appeared, save perhaps as a scribbled note in Mary's or my hand or a hastily assembled list of priorities written before or during each meeting.

Chairwomen were not needed. We all shared each job as it arose, as our talents allowed and our time each week permitted. If one of us was away someone else took over that job. Within a few weeks we became a constant group of ten. We moved in turn from house to house enjoying the comfort and variety of each home. Babies and infants would be brought in carrycots or tucked up in beds, if no babysitters were to be found, and slowly we began to learn a little about each other; but we never asked each other what our husbands did, what our politics or religious beliefs, if any, were or even if we had jobs outside the home. Some of this information naturally emerged in the course of our always animated and often exhausting conversations. We were all mothers – this is still our common bond – with a deep fear for our children's futures hanging in a mushroom cloud above our heads. And the talents we found in each other (all very different women) were too many to count. There were gifted artists, typists and letter writers. There were budding journalists and 'think-tanks'; devil's advocates and those with a clarity of mind when we all became tired, clouded and confused; diplomats, economists and comediennes – and Ingrid, who always had just the right word or phrase. Each one of us assumed all or some of these roles at different times.

We learned a lot about working together as a group. We learned how to take valid criticism without it being seen as a personal attack (though we did lose one mother from the group in this process). We learned to accept that posters might be redrawn and leaflets re-written in our absence. And we tried hard never to undermine each other or put each other down.

We started after that first night with a slogan for a poster which was to become our publicity slogan – CHILDREN NEED SMILES, NOT MISSILES– and we went away to get our children to paint pictures of a smiling child (between us we had twenty children at the last count). The pictures were stunning and hard to choose between but eventually seven-year-old James' large round face was chosen and the process of turning it into a poster began.

We agonised over the lettering – should it be in children's handwriting or was that adult manipulation? Was the publicity to describe the event as a walk for mothers, fathers and children, for parents or for mothers and children only? We all felt that the idea of mothers and children (which was the original idea) had by far the greatest impact, both emotionally and visually; that with men it would look like every other Nuclear Disarmament demonstration; that being mothers would prevent violence or any undesirable infiltration of our walk; and that as mothers we could appeal to many women who like ourselves were politically unsophisticated and who had perhaps never taken part in a 'demonstration' before. We didn't wish, however, to reject caring fathers. This problem has never been satisfactorily resolved, as we are bound to be criticised whoever we choose to include – radical feminists objected to the inclusion of men, and many caring and single-parent fathers resented their exclusion. This year, 1982, we are inviting fathers on our mothers' and childrens' walk. Many hours were spent on this subject rather than a vote being taken!

Then there was the vexed question of the peace symbol ☮ – should it be included on the poster? I didn't realise at that time that this symbol was not exclusive to CND. In the end we felt that many people might think the same way as I did and be put off because of the image they might have of CND. Any idea of some crusading 'sect' had to be avoided (we had just had an insidious 'peace' petition circulated by the 'Moonies' in Oxford – people were cautious). We came to realise that we wanted to appeal to as many mothers as possible, to be a consciousness-raising exercise, a broad umbrella without religious or political affiliations. We left the symbol off the poster, even though some of us thought it should be there.

So that any mother could feel comfortable joining our demonstration, we carefully publicised the event as a calm and gentle 'walk' and emphasised that people were not to bring posters, banners or leaflets, so as to discourage any extreme elements who might have wished to sell or distribute their literature or shout political slogans. We provided a stall with material on all aspects of, and groups within, the peace movement, in the park.

James Lavelle's poster for the first walk

This was just another example of the great care with which every aspect of the walk was treated. The leaflet that we designed and wrote was dealt with in the same way: every sentence was examined for hidden overtones or understatements. There were even times when we began to think that a benign autocrat or dictator would be more efficient than our time-consuming democracy! However, jobs were delegated as time closed in on us. Negotiations for the park ground through the wheels of the local council bureaucracy; entertainers were engaged (almost too late, but a Punch and Judy show – could it be too sexist and violent, *NO*, it's traditional and anyway too late to hire anyone else! – a clown, folk singer, hand puppets and face painting were organised). Insurance for the walk and the park was bought, posters and 20,000 leaflets, some of which had been translated into two locally spoken Asian languages, were printed and distributed by over 100 volunteer mothers and groups throughout the city and surrounding countryside to every primary and infant school, playgroup and nursery, health centre, library and community centre that we could find! Posters were displayed and fly-posted. The leaflets were also distributed in the city centre and outlying shopping centres before the walk.

We patchworked two beautiful banners, OXFORD MOTHERS' WALK FOR NUCLEAR DISARMAMENT, Rhoda wrote numerous letters seeking sponsorship and donations from sympathetic organisations, and Janet and Julia opened a bank account and kept dazzlingly juggled accounts, whereby we raised enough money to cover expenses. We wrote to every magazine, national and local newspaper we could think of, and to *Woman's Hour*, who read our letter over the air. Mary, Rhoda and Judith gave riveting performances on local radio and in articles in the local press, and we fought with (and learnt a great deal from) a local newspaper which printed an inaccurate, distressing and highly sensationalist article. They publicly withdrew their remarks and apologised. We became more competent and confident.

Permission for the route of the walk was sought from the local police and the Chief Superintendent and Chief Inspector were charmed into conceding the best route through Oxford centre on a Saturday afternoon, by Judith in her respectable Burberry mac, myself, a double baby-buggy and two beguilingly unselfconscious two-year-olds with no respect for authority or policemen's laps. They also gave us excellent police support on the day!

Shortly before the day of the walk (26 September 1981), Liz made beautifully hemmed stewards' arm bands, placards were made with some remaining posters backed on to card or hardboard with wooden sticks; Inneke organised a local restaurant to provide a hot food van in the park; and the enormous job of compiling a handout was undertaken – here Scilla's wide experience and knowledge proved invaluable. As there was to be no rally in the park – we didn't want to alarm some of the more impressionable children with the horrors of nuclear war – we decided to give each mother a handout as she entered the park, which briefly outlined why we were worried, listed addresses of other disarmament groups, suggested what we as women and mothers could do, and included a short article by Scilla setting our action in the wider perspective of what women have done and are doing in other parts of the world to combat the nuclear threat.

The day arrived and it rained. A group of about 200–300 mothers and children gathered in the drizzle at 2.30 in St Giles, Oxford, with their babies in pushchairs, and bought brightly coloured helium-filled balloons from a supporter, who organised the blowing up. At three o'clock we set off at a brisk pace through the centre of Oxford, gathering momentum, passers-by and numerous mothers and children on our way through the traffic-stopped streets. One elderly woman in a bus queue with two large shopping bags stepped off the pavement and said she would walk to the next stop. Then, as if to welcome us as we approached the park, a wonderful clown and the sun came out at the same moment to meet us. Nearly 1000 mothers and children were counted as they passed through the gates into the park, including the above-mentioned old lady. 'I came all the way!' she said.

We welcomed the walkers briefly and thanked them, and then we all got on with our picnics, play puppets and entertainment, meeting strangers from all over the country who had come to be with us, to exchange our experiences and ideas. Then we slowly drifted away – exhausted, I went home to celebrate my wedding anniversary and the end of a long day and five months of preparation.

Why We Are Here

These are some of the reasons why we are worried:

1. Britain has more nuclear weapons per square mile than any other country in the world. These include Polaris, Vulcan, and a large American force of nuclear weapons and bombers based in Britain.

2. What we are going to get unless we stop it:

Cruise Cruise missiles are small, pilotless planes which fly close to the ground, evading radar detection, and have great accuracy, striking within 100 feet of their targets after flights up to 1500 miles. Cruise carries a warhead as powerful as 15 Hiroshima bombs. The government has agreed to a NATO plan to deploy 160 Cruise missiles in Britain by 1983–84. They will be stationed at Greenham Common in Berkshire and at Molesworth in Cambridgeshire. In times of international crisis, the missile launchers will be moved out of these bases and dispersed around the country within a radius of up to 100 miles. The accuracy of Cruise makes it ideal for destroying military targets; it is a weapon not for deterring a nuclear attack, but for actually fighting a war – in Europe.

Trident   Trident submarines and missiles are planned to replace Polaris in the early 1990s at a cost of £5,000,000,000. Trident can launch three times as many warheads as Polaris (perhaps more) against Soviet or other cities, and a British Trident fleet could kill 70 million people.

But Trident is a highly accurate missile, its warheads being guided to their targets by satellite. For the purposes of 'deterrence', such accuracy is quite unnecessary, since cities present big targets. Rather, Trident's accuracy makes it suitable for destroying 'hardened' Soviet missile sites *before* their missiles have been launched. This is not a policy of deterrence, but one of counterforce. It could involve us in being the first side to use nuclear weapons (which is, in fact, a prospect that forms part of current NATO strategy). The US is deploying a vast range of highly accurate weapons that may give it the capability to strike first by 1990. The USSR may not reach this point until the year 2000.

3. It is widely accepted that any nuclear war will probably be fought in Europe and that Britain, as an integral base in American defence strategy, is a prime target in a planned attack. American military independence is such that the US Air Force could actually initiate a nuclear war against the USSR from British soil, without the involvement of British Parliament.

Richard Nixon, when President of the United States, commented, 'I can go into my office and pick up the telephone, and in 25 minutes 70 million people will be dead.'

4. In the event of a nuclear exchange, there would be no safe place to take our children. Bomb shelters in cities under attack would be useless, owing to the blast, heat and radiation effects.

Shelters as far as six miles from the centre of even a one-megaton surface nuclear explosion would become ovens for their occupants.

People in Nottingham looking at the fireball of a 15-megaton bomb in London would be blinded.

The government's booklet *Protect and Survive*, which will be distributed to every home in the event of a state of emergency, instructs us to stay in our homes. (Travel will be prohibited, and all exits from cities will be closed.) We are told how to build a Fall-Out room in our cellar, hall or passage with an inner refuge made under tables or with sloping doors 'strengthened' with sandbags, books and clothing. It also instructs us to label corpses and place in another room.

Since this booklet was published, we have listened to the views expressed by scientists and doctors, and feel that their informed and realistic view of the situation is far more plausible.

Doctors and scientists attending the 30th Pugwash Conference 1980 (from at least 14 countries, including the UK, USA and USSR) gave the following warning:

> Effective civil defence against a nuclear attack is impossible . . . Medical disaster-planning for a nuclear war is futile. There is no possible effective medical response after a nuclear attack – in one major city alone, in addition to the hundreds of thousands of sudden deaths, there would be hundreds of thousands of people with severe burns, trauma and radiation sickness – all demanding intensive care. Even if all medical resources were intact, the care of these immediate survivors would be next to impossible. In fact, most hospitals would be destroyed, medical personnel among the dead and injured, most transportation, communication and energy systems inoperable and most medical supplies unavailable. As a result, most of the people requiring medical attention would die.

The United Nations hopes that an 'international conscience will develop and that world public opinion will exercise a positive influence'. In the Final Document adopted by the General Assembly at the Special Session on Disarmament in May 1978, paragraph 15 reads:

> It is essential that not only governments but also the peoples of the world recognise and understand the dangers in the present situation.

And after the walk? We held a follow-up meeting (publicised in our handout) which about a dozen mothers apart from our group attended, where we tried to formulate plans for the future. It was not a success, we were all too mentally exhausted.

We settled our accounts and came out with a little left over in the bank. The day had cost us £246.52. The money to cover our expenses (balloons, insurance, publicity, entertainment) had all come from sponsorship and donations.

We held post-mortems of the event itself and of the success and failures of its organisation. How could we have got more media coverage on the day? (Half a dozen lines in the local newspaper was the sum total – we were described as 'about 250 mothers and children'. The reporter left before we started our walk.)

The autumn was a vacuum in the life of the group – a hiatus, filled with odd unsatisfactory meetings where no direction for our work was discernible. There was a great weariness and an apathy in the group and yet a sense of loss felt by all of us. I think in retrospect this was a period of fallowness that every living organism requires to replenish its energies, to grow anew. Most of us felt we wanted to continue in some way. We didn't want to give up the friendship we now valued.

Some members left us. Inneke felt that the group was too middle-class and that she wanted to attempt to reach more working-class mothers by making personal contacts in her own area. Ingrid left us because, with great honesty and sincerity, she was re-evaluating her ideas on the whole nuclear question, unilateral disarmament in particular.

This individual crisis coincided with a loss of direction in the group: we had formed to organise one event and not to become another peace organisation, yet increasingly we were being called upon to fulfil this function. Some of our difficulties were reflected in our discussions over whether or not to join the Women's Peace Alliance. Was it an umbrella organisation feeding information to a wide range of women's peace groups? Or a radical feminist mouthpiece? Or a political sect? On the whole we viewed the first idea favourably and the latter two with alarm. Feminism, like politics or religion, is a personal matter and has no direct part to play in our mothers' organisation. We did in fact join the Alliance.

Slowly and almost imperceptibly we changed, regrouped and reformed, perhaps more in response to external events. As a group or as individuals we attend and speak at rallies, conferences and peace camps; the whole group went on the 6 June 1982 CND rally, the banner went to the UN Special Session on Disarmament II. Decisions on which events to support are made democratically by discussion within group meetings. We organised another walk for 1982 – 10 July, and more mothers have joined to help. Due to the pressure of these events, of living with young families and the desire not to get sidetracked by the endless self-analysis and internal squabbling that seems to characterise other peace groups, we still have not seriously tackled the problems of who and what we are or of formulating some kind of policy. We recognise these problems but we all feel that the Oxford Mothers for Nuclear Disarmament have a role to play by supporting peace action, gathering and disseminating information, meeting and reaching out to as many mothers as we can, organising an annual walk and encouraging, by our example and with our help, as many individuals and newly formed groups as possible across the country to hold their own, possibly similar, events. As a result of the 1981 walk eight groups in different parts of the country began to organise events or walks of their own. In this way eventually a network of mothers and women's peace groups will spread throughout the country.

8
On Common Ground:
The Women's Peace Camp
at Greenham Common

LYNNE JONES

RAF Greenham Common is one of the intended sites for 96 Cruise missiles in December 1983. (Twenty will be sited at RAF Molesworth in East Anglia in 1986). The missiles will be deployed around the country, in a time of crisis. The women's peace camp has been there since 5 September 1981 as a nonviolent protest against these and all nuclear weapons. At the time of writing, in spite of the eviction mentioned in the chapter, the women continue their action at Greenham Common.

The Beginning

It was cold, dark and wet, the first time that I visited the camp at Greenham, in the November of 1981. I'd heard the stories, legends rather, for that is what they'd become: how a woman called Anne Pettit, living on a smallholding in Wales with her husband and two children, had organised a women's march from Cardiff to RAF Greenham Common to protest against Cruise Missiles. She'd wanted to inspire 'women not necessarily in the women's movement, but who were worried, anxious and isolated like myself'. She called the march WOMEN FOR LIFE ON EARTH to show that it wasn't just a negative protest, and succeeded in inspiring 40 women and four men to join her. They were women like Liz Stocker who'd 'never thought much about the peace thing' and 'didn't think women worked well together in groups'. Liz had seen an advertisement for the march in *Cosmopolitan*. She'd been ill all year and went 'to learn something and see if I could walk that far'. They had walked through sunny countryside and friendly villages 'and in 48 hours', Liz went on 'we had become a very close group; all totally

Church Hall, Newbury. The last morning of the Women's March

Drawing by Sarah Wilson

different backgrounds yet we sorted out our disagreements, cut through the nonessentials with none of the egotripping that you get on male committees'. The media, however, had ignored them, so they'd decided to chain themselves to the perimeter fence of the base, saying that they would stay until there was a live television debate between John Nott, Minister of Defence, and themselves on the issue of Cruise missiles. Nothing happened. The issue had 'already been debated', they were told that they could stay as long as they liked. More and more women had arrived, however, and local people brought tents and food. 'We decided,' Anne told me, 'that while there might not be much point in chains there was a point in having a permanent peace picket. We called it a Women's Peace Camp and decided to stay, and you know, when we came out of the tent there was an enormous Harvest Moon in the sky and a rainbow, good omens.'

There was no rainbow now. Only mud, wet bracken and a huddle of caravans by the main gate of the base. A small shelter had been erected by an open fire, two men sat by it. 'Is anyone around?' I asked. 'Effie's in her caravan, over there.' I knocked on the door, opening it to see a small, frail-looking old lady buried under a heap of blankets. 'Hello,' she mumbled, waking. 'Do come in. It's so cold and I get so tired of making tea for visitors, I though I'd have a rest.

Do sit down.' She pushed a heap of clothes aside. 'I'm sorry it's so untidy, the girls don't seem to mind, would you like tea? They're all away today.' While I drank tea, Effie talked about her grand-children and her market garden. 'We grow tomatoes, shrubs and things. No, I haven't done anything like this before. We're rather remote, you see, we don't have any daily papers but I had begun to realise things were altering. I came because I wanted reassuring. I was one of the ones chained up, you know.'

'What was that like?'

Two women resting during the Women's March

'When it was first mooted, I thought it was dreadful. Cold shadows went through me at the thought, but we discussed it . . . It was freezing cold and the traffic was noisy but I didn't mind.'

'What made you stay?'

'There are so few here, and my husband doesn't mind, we've been married 30 years. He was a CO in the last war. He paid my train fare. Are you staying?'

'Oh Effie, I'm sorry, I can't. I have to be back on duty at the hospital,' I said, feeling guilty.

'Oh well.' Effie looked tired.

'I'll go now,' I said, 'and be down again soon.' I stepped out of the caravan feeling depressed and impressed both at the same time. 'It can't last,' I thought. 'It's too difficult.'

In early December Anne wrote to me, saying 'The camp's going strong. Hundreds of people visit every weekend. Why don't you come down?'

The camp looked different and not just because there were two feet of snow on the ground. Bright signs had been painted saying WOMEN'S PEACE CAMP, NO CRUISE HERE, HONK IF YOU'RE FOR US. There were ten caravans and two teepees. Smoke rose from the fire where about twenty people had gathered around a woman talking. I'd heard of Helen before. She'd caught the media's eye because she'd given up five children, husband and home to live here. She was 44, a midwife and 'asleep like everyone else' until she'd gone to an anti-nuclear rally in Wales. 'Seeing those young people trying desperately to stop their futures being damaged, I realised my generation hadn't worked hard enough to prevent what's happening. It was a fit of guilt that got me going.' Initially she'd joined the Labour party and had stood as a councillor in Powys, her home county, to get the issue raised. Now she felt it was more important to be here. 'People are disillusioned with politics and rightly so. They need something they can focus their attention on and begin to believe in. You can actually draw a line here and make a positive physical statement that cannot be misunderstood: we are not allowing these weapons in. If I'd said it in Powys they wouldn't have listened.' She hadn't planned to take direct action. 'I never disapproved but I thought the way a lot of women with children think, that I'd a greater responsibiltiy to them than what I felt was right for me. The thought that these missiles could kill all the people I cared about anyway changed that. The only logical thing to do was to make a committed stand. I felt I had the right to make that decision on my own without consulting my husband and children. Obviously they were very upset. The youngest is four and my husband has had to give up his job and go on social security, which he hates, though he understands what I'm doing and he supports the peace movement. I just had to decide whether I was going actively to involve myself in this protest or put it aside for someone else to do because of the children. It's one of those decisions that affects the rest of your life – I chose to become involved.'

'Shall we march into Newbury?' she asked us all.

Someone handed out mugs of tea. 'How do you organise yourselves here?' I asked, 'Who makes decisions? How does it run?'

'Chaotically,' Helen said, 'and I think that's our greatest strength in a daft way, we never seem to know what we're doing from day to day, which makes it hard for the authorities to know either. The chaos comes from people coming and going. No one sits down and makes rigid plans, which is excellent or you'd be stuck if something happened fast.'

'Don't you have rotas or anything?'

'Rotas?' Helen spat out the word with a laugh. 'Oh my God! There were rotas but nobody paid attention to them. Somebody had this mania to write them, but nobody took any notice.'

'It doesn't run smoothly all the time,' a small, dark-haired woman called Shushu joined in. 'But mostly it's OK. People simply agree on what needs to be done and do it. We meet most evenings over supper. We don't have a steering committee or hierarchy or all that kind of thing. My CND group did and spent most of its time organising jumble sales and never doing anything.'

'Why did you come?' I asked.

'I've just finished school. I've got the time and energy to do something more than organise jumble sales.'

'Once you've accepted the fact that you can live with a greater degree of untidiness and filth you can relax. I think if we were the type of women who gave a high priority to having clean, smooth-running homes, that's where we'd be. Our priority is stopping Cruise.'

A woman walked up carrying a large puppet; an enormous woman's head with long red hair and brightly coloured hand-painted robes. 'This is the Goddess,' she said.

'Right,' said Helen, 'let's walk to Newbury.'

We set off, the Goddess in the lead, bright against snow-laden branches and clear sky. Sara and I took it in turns to carry the Goddess while she told me about herself. She'd been working in a psychiatric rehabilitation hostel in Sheffield, but hadn't seen the point of trying to help people back to the normality of a society that spent millions of pounds on destroying everything. 'One woman was having nuclear nightmares every night. She couldn't control her normal life at all and kept having tantrums. The social services saw her as not being able to cope with the world so she had to change to fit it. No one said, "You've got good reason to feel like this." Everything that's valued in our society at present is masculine. The heroics, virility, power. It's lunatic and destructive. We've got to work out a more balanced vision where the feminine is valued by everyone. The Women's Peace Camp seemed to combine all the things I'd been working on so I had to come.'

'Was that hard?'

'I knew it was wrong to give up my job and wrong not to come here. They were angry because I was "deserting" them. They thought *I* was crazy coming to live in a teepee in December.'

A Women's Camp
The women continued to camp out through bitter winter weather. Money, letters of support and food poured in and even Newbury people, not naturally sympathetic, as many of them worked in the nuclear industry, began to be impressed. They stopped by the fire on their way to discos on the base; a local policeman left his phone number for anyone wanting baths, and the media came in droves, from Japan, Australia, the States, Europe and the USSR. Meanwhile the women talked. They talked to the workers on the base: Franny ran a one-woman picket outside the construction workers' gate. Sitting with a primus stove she'd hold out a sign saying 'Will you stop and talk?' and another for when they returned saying 'How about a cup of tea on the way back then?' Then she'd ask them what they thought of the men who built the gas chambers in Hitler's Germany, or of Claude Eatherly, the man who flew the weather plane on the Hiroshima mission. 'These men aren't union men, so the only way you can get through is on a personal basis. I just want them to understand what they're doing building a missile site.'

They talked at conferences and meetings all over the world, determined to raise the issue of Cruise missiles. I watched Ev receive a standing ovation from 500 women in Amsterdam when she interrupted a formal conference to tell them about Greenham. One thing the camp was teaching them was to be powerful and effective speakers. 'I'd never have had the confidence to speak at massive rallies before,' Ev said. 'Every time I've been down to the camp I've come away with this great surge of energy, able to do things like set up a Woman's Peace group and get an art show together. Being active helps me confront fear.'

'The point of this camp,' Sarah said, 'is to draw attention to the fact that every day men are helping to build missile silos for the American military forces in this country. Those missiles could trigger off a holocaust. Every day hundreds of people go past on that road and have to ask themselves "What makes those women live here and give up their normal lives?" It's a focus too for all the people in the peace movement, who know what we're up against but are uncertain what to do. They can come here, meet others sympathetic, get inspiration, anything could happen.'

Clearly too much was happening. Another peace camp was set up at RAF Molesworth, the second intended Cruise missile site. The idea was catching. Towards the end of January I read a short column

Do you wonder what I think
as I sit and watch you
come and go along the
country lane?
I see your lorries filled
not with gravel,
but the corpses of my
friends,
as you smile and wave
taking your load
to the tip.
I imagine your anguish
if you survive the bomb
knowing the part
you played.
Wages you earn from the
graves you dig.

If governments didn't
spend our money on
bombs
there would be more
jobs.

Leave this job for
someone elses
conscience

Poem for construction workers by Fran De'ath

in the *Guardian* saying that Newbury District Council had given the women fourteen days to leave or they would be evicted. I had already planned to go down to the camp that weekend to prepare for a festival and nonviolent blockade of the base in March. The threat of eviction brought hundreds of other supporters as well.

A large marquee had been built since my last visit: a circus-like structure of pieces of clear plastic attached to wooden poles around a poplar tree as centre post. A table was covered with leaflets. Banners, appliquées, poems and paintings hung round the walls, smoke rose from the central fireplace where Franny sat dispensing tea to all comers.

'We're going ahead with the festival and blockade whatever happens,' she said.

It wasn't an easy weekend. People couldn't decide whether to focus on the proposed blockade or the eviction. Some felt the women were not providing enough leadership. Underneath all this another difficulty was emerging: the question of Men. A week previously all the women present at the camp had met and unanimously decided that, while under threat of eviction, women only should actually live at the camp. Although up to this point men had been allowed to live there, the march and camp had always been women's initiatives, with women talking to the press, representing the camp and doing the decision-making. Many now felt they should make this position clearer. Others returning the following day were unhappy with the decision, as were the men involved. By Sunday afternoon there was a muttering too loud to ignore and it was going to have to be talked out.

'Men are just as capable of being non-violent as women.'

'Yes, but they often provoke more violence because the police pick on them deliberately.'

'Or they get upset at women being mistreated! It's a tactical decision, we want the authorities to have to deal very clearly with women. Right or wrong it makes them react differently.'

'No one can ask me to leave! We weren't even allowed in the meeting when you made the decision. Anyway this is my home – I've squatter's rights!'

'Cruise missiles are going to affect everyone, not just women.'

'Yeah, you're splitting the peace movement!'

'Do you want a lesbian separatist peace movement? Is that what you want?'

'We want everyone to work in the way they find most effective.'

'Well, some of us women like working in mixed groups.'

'Yes, but some of us don't. We need space to find our own ways of

WOMEN'S PEACE CAMP
Greenham Common

PRESS RELEASE

The women of Greenham Common wish it to be known that as of
Monday 1st.February while the camp is under threat of eviction
only women will be living on the site.This camp has been a
women's led initiative throughout and any actions taking
place on the site will be made by women.

We intend to maintain this camp peacefully and act at all
times in a non violent manner and diffuse confrontation.Men
are welcome to continue their support for us off site and to
keep in contact with us as to the most appropriate ways to do
this.

We intend to deal with women representatives of the
authorities and wish to communicate our actions through
women in the media.We would appreciate it if the press would
respect this request.

'Together we can help create the climate for peace that
the warmongers won't be able to ignore.'

WOMEN'S PEACE CAMP   GREENHAM COMMON   nr.NEWBURY   BERKS

We need as many women as possible at Greenham Common
The peace camp welcomes all women

Support us by publicising this information

working. They seem to be different. More concerned with personal things – feelings and trust and cooperation, not power-tripping . . .'

'. . . and we need space to find our strengths, how to assert ourselves, make speeches and so on – we don't do that in mixed groups.'

'Mixed groups are men's groups, only no one calls them that,'

'Have one man here and it's just assumed the good ideas are his.'

'Us getting strong can only make the peace movement stronger, not split it.'

'If your ways are so good, why don't you let us stay and learn from you?'

'Couldn't you be more useful somewhere else?'

'Start another peace camp!'

'I think behind every good woman there should be a good man!'

'Well! My CND group has always supported Greenham. They'd be very upset to hear you'd gone separatist!'

'There's not much women can call their own. It's important for other women to see Greenham as an initiative successfully taken by women. That gives them hope and pride in their own sex, and encourages them to act as well.'

'But does it stop Cruise missiles?'

'Look, if you, the men, really support us, why can't you support our decision?'

Voices were rising. It was obvious that we were too large a crowd and feelings too strong to reach an agreement. So all the people actually living at the camp at that time went into a caravan and somehow, with the pressure of all of us waiting outside, reached an agreement. Women only for two weeks, then the decision would be reviewed.

The two weeks passed and the decision was reviewed and confirmed. 'It was the best decision we ever made,' said Shushu at a much later date. 'The men were a problem. They put us in the role of mothers. "Mummy show me how to do this", and always pushing to see how far they could go.'

Helen agreed. 'The men are so ludicrously protective. When we first talked of Direct Action on the march, they said guard dogs would be set on us! We'd be abused! One chappie wanted us to walk peacefully up to the gate, hand in a posy of flowers and with quiet dignity disappear into the sunset. That's just what we'd have done, disappear, having wasted ten days of our lives. They simply don't think the same way!'

Not everyone was happy though. 'I don't think we analysed the problem properly,' said Franny. 'Which was those particular men.

None of us had the guts to say, "Shape up or piss off". When the decision was reviewed, those that disagreed weren't there. It wasn't humane either. People were turning up at night in the dark and in the rain, and having to leave. I felt we were a strong enough group to cope with that and not stick to rigid rules.'

'So why did you stay on?' I asked.

'The women felt so strongly about it. Besides, there was the blockade.'

The Blockade

'Isn't this getting a little ridiculous?' the policeman asked. 'How many more of you want to get arrested?' Ridiculous to you perhaps, I thought, to me it seems like the most sensible thing I've ever done in my life.

'We don't want to get arrested. That's not why we're here. We're blocking all the entrances to this camp for 24 hours to show we intend to close it down, because we object to what's going on in there. If you choose to arrest us, that is your affair.'

It was 2.00 p.m. on a Monday afternoon in March, the first warm day of the year. We stood on a quiet country road, Newbury Church just visible over the horizon, the hedges and trees just touched by a green mist, a lark singing, high and clear, peace. For the third time that afternoon women lay down head to toe to fill a gap in the wire fence enclosing the base . . .

I'd been nervous about the blockade. We'd talked about it for weeks. It was to follow on from a festival to celebrate the Spring Equinox. While plans for the festival had gone smoothly ahead, because of concern over the threatened eviction we'd done little to prepare for the blockade. So I had arrived at the camp two days previously with a sick feeling in my stomach that we were heading for disaster. 'Don't worry Lynne,' Shushu had smiled, patting my shoulder, 'We're very organised.' And indeed they had been. One group of women had written a small practical briefing, outlining how the blockade would proceed, what to do if arrested, solicitors' phone numbers and so on. A system had been devised whereby every woman involved in the action would register and join a group to do non-violence training. Each gate into the base would have a legal observer who would watch what happened, note the arrests, and relay information to a central point, via walkie-talkies hired for the purpose. All the previous afternoon women had sat huddled in caravans getting to know one another, and deciding how we'd deal with confrontation. Outside the festival had surged around, tap

Women forming human chain on the blockade at RAF Greenham Common, 22 March 1981

dancers in radiation suits, jugglers, clowns, the Fall-Out Marching Band, all undaunted by the miserable weather. Then I had watched with amazement as 200 women in the space of an hour managed to work out how to cover seven gates for 24 hours, sleep, eat and communicate. It was going to work!

That didn't mean that I wasn't scared as my group walked out to fill the main gate at 6.30 p.m.: a line of police behind an enormous crowd in front and camera lights glaring in our eyes. We sat down. At six other gates women were doing the same thing, and we waited. The rain poured down steadily but the stream of traffic was absent. The base, it seemed, in consideration of our wishes, had closed itself down. So we settled in, wrapped in rugs and macs, and took turns throughout the night to do four-hour shifts. The camermen went home. The rain turned to drizzle. Supporters brought hot tea, and entertainers, left over from the festival, went from gate to gate with fiddles and guitars.

Then in the morning, we discovered the base intended to work as usual. The police had created a new gate on a deserted bit of road. Realising that this made the rest of our blockade meaningless, some from each gate trekked round there.

'This,' the police inspector said, 'is our gate and if you sit in it you will be arrested.' He was very courteous and gave us five minutes to think. The decision was unanimous and the first group of women sat down.

. . . The afternoon wore on. I sat in the dust at the side of the road, sun hot on my face. A line of some thirty women sat opposite me. A line of police faced them. They had changed their tactics and stopped arresting us. They were letting the traffic pile up, then swooping down and pulling us out of the way, letting us back when the traffic had passed. We had changed our tactics too. Five women were too easy to move so as many as possible had formed a strong chain. It was a wearying process. Traffic, mostly gravel trucks, came through every half hour. We were getting good at going limp but it only slowed them down. There'd been some rough treatment: pulled hair, a woman thrown to the ground, but on the whole the police had been friendly, one even sharing his fears about nuclear war with us. Two women were keening, they had done so steadily all afternoon, wailing, 'No more war, this isn't a game, think what you're doing.'

'We were determined,' Sarah said later, 'that our vision, not theirs, should be in control of that space.'

It was growing cold, sun low and red in the sky, the police were pulling barbed wire back across the gap, they were leaving. All the

Women talking to police at the blockade at RAF Greenham Common, 22 March 1981

women started shouting and hugging each other. 'We've done it! We've done it.' Singing and dancing we formed a circle. Then suddenly, spontaneously, silence fell. We stood filling the road. A policeman giggled, but then muffled his radio. They were silent too, for the first time that afternoon with us, not against us.

'Pass a smile around,' a woman whispered in my ear grinning. I whispered to my neighbour and watched as the women's faces lit up.

A letter in *Peace News* the following week read:

'The blockade' as a blockade was a failure and . . . I would say that what I saw symbolically, and actively, manifested was woman's oppression and subjugation . . . they were using their bodies the way they've been used for centuries, lumps of unintelligent flesh booted aside when they got in the way. No attempt was made to seal off the site in a proper pacifist way with glue, padlocks and chains . . .

Angered, I wrote back:

. . . What mattered was the effect that symbol had on ourselves and the people we were confronting. A policeman tryng to pull two arms apart in a firmly linked human chain has to directly confront his own feelings about human contact, handling women not as sexual objects but as powerful beings . . . hacking through a chain he can avoid all that. It's just the nice easy masculine field of mechanics, no feelings involved. It's that objectification, that lack of understanding as to what pain and suffering really mean that makes it possible to press a button and annihilate a million people, that's what we're trying to challenge. That action meant directly confronting these people with our bodies . . . with the comprehension of what violence and power mean in human terms . . . No, we didn't 'win', but you can't take control till you feel powerful and not one of us left that day without feeling stronger and more sure of our power to act. Surely not the result of a day of oppression and subjugation.

Two days later I handed in my resignation at the hospital where I was working. Helen rang me up. 'Lynne! You can't give up your job. We need doctors.'

'I consider nuclear weapons a health threat and I'm not confronting it here in casualty. You're a fine one to talk anyway. Have you been evicted yet?'

'Not yet, they're applying for a court order. We'll get five days' notice to prepare our case.'

'How's Franny?'

'She's set up a new camp at the construction gate – mixed. Come and see us.'

The Eviction

April – the camp looked beautiful. The poplar in the centre of the marquee was sprouting fresh green leaves. Blackthorn blossomed in the hedges. I stood by the for once unlit fire. 'Hello,' a voice shouted. Looking up, Sara's grinning face was just visible through a hole in the roof. 'We're building a tree house for when they evict us. It rests on the structure so they can't take that down without risking our lives.'

'Brilliant!' I said.

Another woman was making a rope ladder, and another binding rushes together. 'For walls,' she said. 'They come from the Kennett near Silbury Hill, did you know the land is sculptured in the female form?'

'No, I didn't. Who are you?'

'Since I've come down here I've called myself Ioma Axe.'

'Hello Lynne,' said Shushu, 'Did you hear about our flying blockades?'

'We've developed a new technique, small blockades as and when it suits us. We did one to greet a visiting American General,' Helen added.

'It only ended when an American Serviceman tried to psych us out by revving up his bike and it burst into flames between his legs. He was OK,' Shushu went on.

'That's what convinced me I had to stay,' Io said. 'Magic.'

'Had you been down before?'

'For the blockade on the 21st and the atmosphere was so good – spider webs woven everywhere and all these different women, Buddhist nuns, women from France, all working together. I just thought "This is it! This is the place!" She laughed. 'I've had a lot of asthma and before the weekend I'd thought "I'll probably get pneumonia and die." Then I found myself saying, "go and do it – you're not going to die and if you do – tough!".'

A small child ran by, a woman spoke to him in German. 'That's Beatrice,' said Helen. We wandered out on to the grass verge where a star, made from branches and wool woven together, swung in the breeze.

'Do you think the camp has changed?'

'Yes, you've got a lot of women coming now who are much more involved in the women's movement, committed to feminist principles. They're also much clearer on the nuclear issues.'

I noticed a small spiral of painted rocks on the grass. 'We've started a peace cairn here and at the construction gate,' Sara told me. 'So that people who can't be here can show they care by leaving a rock, that way they see they're not alone. Rocks and stones are the oldest things. They have a lot of power.'

Small signs had appeared around the camp: ASK PEOPLE WHO THEY ARE, DON'T GIVE YOUR NAME TO STRANGERS.

'The council have been up here looking around,' said Shushu.

Two weeks later a letter arrived from Annie. The council was going to the high court on the 14th of May for an 'Order to recover possession of the land at Greenham Common'. The case rested on the fact that we had broken minor bye-laws. I noticed that one of the bye-laws applying to the common stated that no person 'should throw or discharge missiles'. Some nineteen named defendants and persons unknown were also summoned to say why they shouldn't be evicted.

The court hearing, as we expected, went against us. We spent the night of the 14th blockading the main gate, hourly expecting the bailiffs. The eviction didn't occur that night however, or the next.

The blockade of the main gate continued, women came from all over the country, bringing food, staying a day. We gradually prepared the camp, moving stuff we didn't want to lose and most of our caravans on to a small strip of Ministry of Transport land 100 yards from the main gate. It was wearying, waiting, difficult to keep the fire going or our energy levels high.

On Thursday 27 May, when I had gone home for a few days, a friend phoned. 'They've been evicted.' I turned on the six o'clock news in time to see Sara being lifted bodily from the cab of a bulldozer.

It took them nine hours to raze the camp to the ground, doing considerable damage to our poplar tree in the process, giving Beatrice mild concussion and arresting five women for causing a breach of the peace in the process. They left the caravans on the Ministry of Transport land alone.

I am sitting in court with twenty to thirty other women filling the benches beside me. Clutching handfuls of flowers, dressed in bright clothing, they are the most cheerful sights there. Three magistrates: two women and one man, straight-faced and neatly pressed, gaze down on Io, Tina, Amanda and Beatrice in the dock, who are surrounded by police. They all look rumpled, having spent the night in the cells, but that didn't stop Sara and Beatrice from bursting into the court singing their lungs out and embracing all the women within reach before being hustled into the dock.

We've listened for two hours to the witnesses for the prosecution, mainly police officers, read from their notebooks as to how the defendants lay or stood in front of a bulldozer, while other women walked round it 'tying it up with string'. The assistant bailiff has complained of being followed around by 'ladies singing', and has told us that 'It wasn't for us to decide what was what, ours was to obey orders'.

'At what point does anyone take responsibility?' Sara asks from the witness stand. She is speaking in her own defence and has already confused the clerk by stating that she finds the oath acceptable if she may swear on the Goddess, rather than God.

'We are all of us intelligent people. How can we sit around hiding the truth, talking legal jargon. We could all be sitting together using our hearts and minds to deal with the terrible situation we face. Even if you feel that the possibility of a holocaust is remote, why does everyone refuse to discuss it. Today we have heard the bailiff say that he was only doing his job, the reasons for the peace camp being at Greenham Common are not his concern. The police say they are only doing their job because they are asked to by the bailiff. The court is here today because the police have brought us here . . .

'I am charged with disturbing the peace. My whole life is dedicated to peace. I may sing loudly but I do not swear or abuse anyone, I am totally non-violent. I do not eat meat, harm any person or animal on this planet. I try to find harmony with the earth, my cycles with the cycles of the moon and planets. I search for peace in a world which prepares for war.'

Ioma, Tina and Beatrice follow, reiterating Sara's points. Beside me Jane is weaving a web across the palm of her hand and behind me I can hear humming. The solicitor speaks in Amanda's defence.

'At no point did my client show any violent resistance. I think my client would say that the idea of the Queen's Peace comes from the King's Peace defined during the civil war, not just in the narrow sense as meaning law and order but as a state of affairs where all can live peacefully.'

How can one get through to them? They sit on the bench, expressionless, unmoved. The clerk rises. 'We ask you to enter a recognisance to keep the Queen's Peace for the next twelve months for the sum of £25. Are you willing to so enter?' He asks each in turn.

'No,' says Amanda quietly.

'I follow my own morality as I always have. If these people continue what they are doing I shall continue what I am doing,' Sara replies.

'Is that no?' the clerk asks in a tired voice.

'I must follow my own morality.'

'I think we must take that as no. Ioma Axe?'

'I do not accept your wording or your values. I believe I always have kept the peace.'

'Will you answer the question, yes or no!'

'No,' says Io.

'Yes, I will keep the peace as I always have,' says Beatrice.

'You may stand down,' the clerk says, in a relieved voice, choosing to misunderstand her.

'I'll use my own interpretation of the word peace,' says Tina.

'You MUST answer the question,' the clerk almost shouts in exasperation. 'Yes or no!'

'I'll use my own interpretation,' Tina stands her ground.

'Then I must ask the court to decide.' Red-faced, the clerk sits down.

The magistrates confer, the humming grows louder. 'That's all we're living for, to try and keep the peace!' Jane cries out to the magistrates. 'The rules of this court don't seem adequate to deal with the subject matter in hand.' Helen states in a matter of fact tone, 'They're living it on a daily basis.' Jane continues, 'Can't you see that? You must stop hiding behind that book and have courage!'

'Seven days,' mutters one of the lady magistrates, scarcely looking up.

We're sitting on the steps outside the court, waiting for the van taking them to Holloway to drive by. Jane is still weaving wool, the children are asleep. As to the future? We believe in it. Jane told me this morning that they left the peace cairn alone. Women are planning to come back, and there are peace camps outside military bases all over the country now: Lakenheath, Faslane, Molesworth, Fairford, Caerwent, Burtonwood, Burghfield, Waddington, Upper Heyford . . . We aren't going away. We'll be there for as long as it takes.

9

At the Foot of the Mountain:
The Shibokusa women of Kita Fuji

LEONIE CALDECOTT

The wind blows low on the mountain:
The image of decay.
Thus the superior woman stirs up the people
And strengthens their spirit.

> (from the *I Ching*, with slight liberty of gender)

I am one of those who have never known war. Nor have I tasted poverty, nor physical disability, nor grief beyond endurance. I grew up in the privileged Europe of the fifties, sixties and seventies. A Europe at peace. And yet I have never known peace. Anaesthesia yes; peace no.

Eco-feminists often speak of the violence which permeates the world, making connections between rape and militarism, pornography and pollution, competition and Cruise missiles. I see those connections, I follow the evil spark as it burns its way from one to another, showing its face over and over, everywhere I look. But the face of violence with which I am most familiar is a shadowy, elusive one, hard to hold at arm's length and denounce, because it has made a home inside my life: it is the violence of despair, resignation, powerlessness. The violence of the lie you can never quite pin down. The knowledge that something is wrong, but so deeply wrong that others would rather call it right, or natural, or real.

All through my childhood and adolescence, I struggled to adjust my set to that reality, to that invisible violence. I don't know where the interference came from, but it came, in longer and longer waves, hissing and crackling that all was not right even in this comfortable, well-fed world of mine. That even though no soldiers with machine guns knocked on my door at the dead of night, I was still under siege from the heavy paternal hand closing gently (how subtle are its ways!) and inexorably around my identity, my understanding, my actions. Even though I had freedom of speech, a voice kept trying to speak through me, justifying itself in a litany of inevitability and 'realism', proclaiming that violence is the way of humanity, until kingdom come, and that everything hinges on this.

I could either allow myself to be crushed and moulded by this logic, or I could hold out against it. In order to do the former, I would have had to numb that part of myself which instinctively cried out under its weight. In order to do the latter, I needed to create space in which to let my true self breathe and develop. I did this first by becoming a writer, and then by involving myself in feminism and the peace movement, throwing my lot in with women who were learning to do without the anaesthetic security of the patriarchal mould. It is not an exaggeration to say that being with and writing about these women has been the strongest factor in keeping me from subsiding back into passive despair.

I feel now that my life is an act of defiance, a challenge to come up with something surprising. I find myself in pursuit of the quality of life which constitutes peace in the fullest sense, not merely, as Martin Luther King put it, the absence of tension. This peace has everything to do with tension, but nothing to do with deadlock. It is a peace which springs from human creativity, from people who think and act in their own name, and not in accordance with some other authority, who cooperate with each other because they understand the needs of others as well as their own. I have turned from regretting the impossible to stalking the possible.

In many ways, my own story could not be more different from that of the Shibokusa women of Mount Fuji. They have lived all their lives in a rural Japanese community in which women were not so long ago (and perhaps still) treated little better than cattle, sitting on the ground while their menfolk occupied the *Tatami* mat, eating the leftovers after the men had been fed. They gave birth in the straw. I, on the other hand, have been brought up on the other side of the world, in a wealthy western city, in a culture where women have nominal equality and give birth, more often than not, hooked up to a formidable array of sophisticated technology within the sanitised confines of hospitals. The women of Kita Fuji (North Fuji) have struggled for centuries to eke a living from the land. My own closest contact with the land has consisted of a few hours gardening in my 'spare' time and a heartfelt, if rather abstract, attachment to whatever rural landscape still remains outside my city environment. I can afford the luxury of romanticising the countryside, because my hands are not plunged into it.

The hands of the Shibokusa women are worn and leathery from their labours. The only such mark on my own hand is an occasional dryness which comes from contact with detergents, and a slight callous on the middle finger of the right hand, which comes from holding a pen. I sit indoors for much of the time in order to earn my living. I have had every educational advantage whereas, even now, many of the Shibokusa women cannot read or write. They live most of their lives out of doors; in winter the temperature drops up to twenty degrees below freezing.

It was in winter – the sixth of December 1981 – that I first met the Shibokusa women. It was also in an environment to which neither of us belonged: the teeming megalopolis of Tokyo. I had come to Japan, for the first time in my life, to address a Japanese women's peace rally about the European peace movement and women's initiatives within it. It also happened that this was the first major rally at which I had ever spoken. That it had been organised by women was very exciting to me. After the rally 2,500 of us marched through the towering, modern blocks of Tokyo's commercial district, behind a banner declaring: 'We will not allow the way towards war!' As I marched in their midst, I felt like Gulliver in Lilliput – the only European and at least a head taller than most of them. Yet these proud, jubilant women chanting 'No more Hiroshima! No more Nagasaki! No more Bikini!' and *Onnanatadé Héva*! ('Women for Peace!') more than made up for their lack of physical stature with their infectious sense of determination. At that point the Japanese peace movement had not yet reached its new peak (which resulted in nearly half a million people demonstrating in Tokyo six months later). I got the distinct impression that women had played a large part in keeping the movement alive during its bleak period.

This is hardly surprising when you look at the Shibokusa women. When they got up at the women's rally, dressed in traditional peasant cotton trousers and jacket and wide straw hat – four of them holding their banner and one of them delivering an impassioned, angry speech against the military – I almost jumped out of my seat. Next to their heart-felt and evident emotion, the rest of the speeches paled into insignificance. Excitedly, I asked Yumiko Jansson, who had translated my own speech into Japanese and was acting as my interpreter, who these women were. She explained that their land, which was at the north foot of Mount Fuji, was being used by the Japanese self-defence force (Japan is not supposed to have an army as such) for military exercises, and that some of the women in the area had established a resistance movement to protest against this. My mind's eye leapt out of the city to the foot of the mountain. I had to get up there and talk to those women.

Shumiko Shimizu, secretary general of the Japan Women's Council, who were arranging my programme in Japan, liaised with the *Shibokusa Hahano Kai* (Shibokusa Mothers' Committee) to which the women belonged, and made a date to visit them a week later, accompanying me herself and explaining a good deal of the background to their struggle during the two-hour bus journey between Tokyo and Mount Fuji. Yumiko Jansson, who came along as interpreter, was as curious about the women as I was. If it hadn't been for her sympathetic and quick-witted translation (for neither Mrs Shimizu nor the Shibokusa women spoke English) I should have lost a great deal of the detail in their story, not to mention the spirit and humour with which it was told.

We got off the bus in Fuji Yoshida City, the cold winter air sharp in our nostrils and the graceful snow-covered contours of Mount Fuji rising above us. The town looked well kept and prosperous. Mrs Shimizu explained that it used to be two small towns, but had been amalgamated into one and developed with the help of money that inevitably follows the presence of military in a civilian area. The irony of this pattern – material prosperity blinding people to the growing dangers of authoritarian power over them – was a recurring motif during my Japanese trip.

A taxi took us outside the town and down a dirt track through some woods, the mountain lying ahead of us. We soon came to the perimeter of the military base; right next to the gate leading into it, there was a cottage enclosed in a small compound. It is from here, said Mrs Shimizu, that the Shibokusa women coordinate their resistance activities. They take it in turn – in shifts of two – to maintain a presence in the cottage. That day I met four of them, two of whom had stayed on from the previous shift. One of them, Mie Amano, acted as spokeswoman, the other three, including their leader, Kimie Watanabe, occasionally adding a few words of their own. Many of the women I met in Japan still worked in this fairly organised, heirarchical manner. They didn't necessarily fit into the patterns I was used to as a Western feminist. The noticeable thing about Kimie Watanabe however was that although she was designated 'leader' during the bulk of our conversation she remained silent, sitting upright and attentive, occcasionally nodding and smiling at what Mie Amano said.

As we walked into the compound where the cottage stood, I saw that the thatch on the roof had been covered with shiny sheets of corrugated metal. Mie Amano, noticing our inquiring glances, told us that right-wing groups had started harrassing the women, gathering outside the cottage with taunts and cries of 'go home you old witches!', throwing stones and burning brands. The women, afraid that the thatch would catch fire, had been forced to cover it. Other precautions were in evidence as well – bits of barbed wire on the walls of the compound, and even two young lads from the village who had been brought in to protect the women should the need arise. Whatever the implications of all this for a believer in non-violent resistance, I thought as I stepped into the tiny cottage and removed my shoes, these women had obviously touched a raw nerve somewhere! They could hardly be dismissed as insignificant.

Inside the cottage, we all sat around a low table covered in a heavy cloth. Instead of kneeling in the usual Japanese position, with my feet tucked under my body, I was motioned to stretch my legs out under the table. To my astonishment, the area sealed in by the heavy table cloth was heated, a comforting thing on that bitterly cold winter day. The women produced what Yumiko told me were a great delicacy for us to eat: small packets of rice and red bean wrapped in a wafer-thin piece of dark green seaweed. Lots of good protein, vitamins and iron, I told myself firmly as I began to nibble one, and soon started to enjoy it.

During the conversation that followed, I began to piece together the story of the Shibokusa women. The land which lay between the cottage and the mountain had been used by the local people since the Edo period – around the seventeenth century. This was called *Iriaiken*, the right of common people to cultivate and earn a living from a certain place – in this case the Shibokusa area. It was in fact rather poor land, but years of work had enabled them to grow beans and radish there, and even create a silkwork industry. Then in 1936, the militarisation of Japan came to disrupt the fragile prosperity of the community: the army began to execute drills on the Shibokusa land. After the war, the US army stationed troops on the site, which, say the Shibokusa women, led to a startling increase in prostitution in the area. 'We women were treated like the dust on the ground,' says Mie Amano. Even after the 1952 San Francisco Peace Treaty was signed between Japan and the US, the land was not released by the military. Finally on 20 June 1955, seventy farmers staged a protest on the Shibokusa land. 'We were arrested as rioters,' says Mie Amano, 'but as they were taking us by jeep to Fuji Yoshida, the jeep crashed and the chief of police was killed . . . It was an accident, but it drew attention to what we had been doing. Officials from Tokyo came and promised us another 50 hectares of land in compensation for some people who had lost their livelihood, and these people planted pine trees on it. Now that the trees are fully grown, the government claims it is state land again. Really, we are treated little better than slaves.'

Because of the poverty of the land, men in the area have tended to go away to find work, leaving the subsistence-level cultivation to

Shibokusa women on Women's Peace Rally in Tokyo, 1981

the women – all the more so since the loss of the Shibokusa area to the military. And so the women took over the struggle, building a series of cottages on or around the military base and occupying them, small bastions of ordinary life amid the soldiers' incessant preparations for death. The cottage I was sitting in, listening to their story with the hens pecking the ground outside and the steaming pot of green tea on the table, was the fifteenth one they had built.

In 1970, 1000 riot police turned up to evict a small group of women from one of these cottages. 'We were determined to die rather than move,' recalls Mie Amano. 'We had dressed ourselves in the appropriate way to face death – all in white. Lots of people turned up, expecting to see bloodshed: we'd threatened to blow ourselves and the police up with some unexploded grenades we found on the base. But at the last minute Kimie Watanabe said that in fact our dying would serve no purpose, and that if we remained alive we could go on resisting, building new cottages, not letting anyone forget about us. So we surrendered.'

This was a crucial turning point. Once you have faced death and accepted it, but decided to go on living, many fears and anxieties lose their power over you. The Shibokusa women have, in a sense, nothing to lose, and this is what makes them strong. 'Many people in the town have been bought off by the authorities,' says Mie Amano. 'They are comfortable and can't see anything wrong with the way this land is being used. They despise us and treat us with contempt. So we are not only struggling against the government and the military, but against attitudes which we have to confront every day. If there were not people in the outside world who supported us' – and here she bowed to Mrs Shimizu – 'we should not be able to continue this fight. We also try to combat local corruption – making sure that people don't get bribed to vote a certain way in local elections, for instance.'

The Shibokusa women make it their business to disrupt military exercises. In groups of up to ten, they make their way into the exercise area (there are a host of routes, they say, the secret of which they keep to themselves), crawling around the undergrowth and popping up in the middle of the firing. They plant scarecrows to decoy the troops. Sometimes they'll build a fire and sit round it singing and clapping their hands, totally ignoring officials who try to move them on. They are frequently arrested and taken to the police station. 'They are quite gentle, because they are afraid of provoking us – they hate it when we start screaming, and the police have realised that though we are physically easier to arrest than men, we're more trouble afterwards! Men put up a fight, but once it's over they just give everything away. We never give our name, age or anything. We just say we're so old, we can't remember when we were born or who we are . . .'

Indeed most of them are in their late fifties and sixties, or older. They say that by taking on the struggle themselves, they free younger women for child-rearing or other work. 'If anything happens to us, it's not a disaster. The younger ones could soon take our place.'

I asked Mie Amano what they hoped to achieve in the long run. She answered that it now went much deeper than the desire to get their land back. 'As we carried on with our campaign, we realised that the whole phenomenon of militarism is violence against the land, wherever it takes place. So we are really a part of the wider anti-war movement. You see, Mount Fuji is the symbol of Japan. If they are preparing war on her flanks, how can they say Japan desires peace?'

Before leaving, I went outside the compound to take photographs and to gaze through the fence at the mountain. I felt as though I could never have my fill of that sight, and understood at last why Japanese artists have never tired of drawing it. One of the Shibokusa women tugged at my sleeve and pointed into the tall grass a little way from where we were standing. A Japanese soldier crouched there, taking photographs of us with a telescopic lens. I recalled the women in Tokyo pointing out two men taking photographs during the demonstration the week before, telling me they were not from the press. I had pointed my own camera at them, and the men had turned away, embarrassed. Now it didn't seem to matter. Let then know who we are, I thought, let us stand up and be counted. The women were laughing at the soldier. I noticed that Mie Amano's plump, tanned face was criss-crossed with laughter lines. She had a distinctly mischievous look about her.

'Don't imagine our lives are miserable,' she said, nodding emphatically as Yumiko translated. 'It's fun to make a nuisance of ourselves and embarrass those men. This work is our whole life – we enjoy every minute, but we're not lazy about it. This kind of long-term resistance is the first of its kind in Japan. We will continue it to the end. I have seen time and time again how Japanese men will not endure the worst: they have no patience, they give up or get violent, rather than sitting it out.'

She folded her arms in her sleeves and faced the mountain. 'This land used to be green, but they have destroyed so much vegetation with their explosions . . . A lot of grass and bushes were also removed to prevent us having cover for our activities!'

The camp at the foot of Mount Fuji

I asked her whether there were ever moments when they felt it was hopeless. She thought for a minute and then replied.

'We are not clever, most of us have hardly been educated at all. But we are strong because we are close to the earth and we know what matters. Our conviction that the military is wrong is unshakeable.' She waved her arm at the others, blinking their eyes in the winter sun, and laughed. 'We are the strongest women in Japan! And we want other women to be like us.'

I too laughed, and we bowed to one another, Japanese style. It was much more than a polite formality. I salute your spirit, sister, mother, warrior against war.

10
Notes on Organising a Decentralised
International Action –
A Women's Day
for Disarmament

MARGOT MILLER
and LYNNE JONES

Steps in Organisation	The Reality
1. Formulate idea	The initial idea for a decentralised European women's day of action for peace just emerged out of conversation between Dutch women and myself in April 1981. Over the next two months – through meetings on the Copenhagen–Paris march and large amounts of correspondence between a self-appointed group of international contacts – a formal proposal took shape. That was the easy part.

A Women's Day of Action for Peace

A Draft Proposal for Discussion – circulated autumn 1981
Life on earth is in danger. Every day the size of the nuclear arsenal grows and the threat of total destruction comes closer. Women in Europe feel this deeply, they perceive the threat and understand the connection between the violence of militarism and the violence we face every day in our streets, and countryside and homes. We see that we have no control over our own lives but that power lies in the hands of a few shortsighted men. And we feel powerless. But that is changing – we are looking to ways to be powerful and take back control of our lives. We have walked from Copenhagen to Paris to show how we feel, we have met in small groups, held rallies, vigils, fasts – all the time searching for ways of acting EFFECTIVELY.

With this in mind 40 women from 11 different countries met at the end of the march to discuss what we as women could do. We wanted an action that would demonstrate to ourselves and to the rest of society just how powerful we are; that could be organised in a decentralised, democratic, nonhierarchical way; and that would not only be consciousness raising, but would demonstrate the possibilities of effective action. A powerful way of attacking a system that threatens to kill you is not to cooperate with it, but instead to spend that time cooperating with each other and providing the kind of life we as women would like. We therefore propose a WOMEN'S DAY OF ACTION FOR PEACE organised on the SAME day across Europe, a day when women take the day off from their normal activities, both at home and at work, and spend the day in action for Peace.

How would it be organised?
The most important thing is that this is local grassroots action in an international European context. There is already a widespread network of women's groups working for Peace and it is to be hoped that the action could be organised by and through them in their own way in their own area.

Contact with other women could be made by working through the established peace organisations, political women's organisations, trade unions, schools, education centres, women-dominated workplaces, door to door action etc. Solidarity would come from knowing that women all over Europe were taking action on the same day. This would mean that participants in the action could make it relevant to the places where they lived and worked. Nor would it require expensive travelling. Obviously some kind of international coordination would be essential to exchange ideas and information, to concern itself with publicity and fundraising.

How would the day be spent?
This is to be a positive day. The action is to express our hope for the future as much as our criticisms of the present. We feel that there should be no rigid rules, we would hope that all women would contribute as much as they felt able. Taking the day off work, either paid work or work that is done at home, is a strong way of demonstrating how much women contribute. But some women may feel that it is necessary to continue work – doctors and nurses etc. Therefore it was suggested that all women supporting this day should wear armbands as a symbol of support. Visibility is very important and another suggestion is that women at home should for instance, hang blankets out of their windows to show their involvement.

The day could be spent in many activities all organised by women; Festivals, theatre, educational activities – discussions, workshops, rallies, vigils and hunger strikes, all depending on what was appropriate in one's area. Possibly exchanges could be arranged between women of different countries for that day. Another suggestion is that each local group should send letters on that day to women in Eastern Europe and the USSR.

Children should be involved. It is important to sensitise them to this issue and alternative activities could be organised in or outside school around the subject of peace.

What would we hope to gain?
1. Women would feel empowered, having demonstrated to themselves and the rest of society what they contribute and what they can organise if they choose to do so.
2. European connections and solidarity would be increased by this united action.
3. The publicity from such an action and the activities of the day itself would be consciousness-raising on a large scale (as would the preparations beforehand).
4. It is hoped that the size of such an action would be enough to make governments take notice of:
(a) The strength of feeling against armaments.
(b) The preparedness of women to act directly on this issue should the need arise.
(c) It is to be hoped also that the idea will spread and the day could act as a demonstration of what might be possible on a far greater scale for a longer period of time if necessary.

---

2. Circulate it
   Use any networks available. International conferences and actions provide opportunities for discussion, so do journals such as *Disarmament Campaigns, END Bulletin, Peace News* etc.

3. Formulate according to feed-back.

4. Establish international co-ordinating group, i.e. a contact in each country who will let all the other countries know what is going on in her own. Allow at least one month for two-way correspondence.

This group changed over time as some lost enthusiasm and some got more involved.

5. Establish group to co-ordinate nationally.

I failed to do this, thinking such a group would emerge spon-taneously in response to the idea, if it was good enough to be taken up.

6. Circulate nationally
   Use media – straight
                  – alternative
                  – Peace press
   Use *all* available networks
   – women's organisations
   – trade unions
   – churches
   – students
   Speak, write, telephone.

7. Deal with response
   If *poor* – abandon the idea at this stage and inform those who have responded.
   If *good* – follow up with detailed plans for action; i.e. what is expected of local groups/individuals, what national coordination you can provide. We asked local groups to:
   – tell us what they were planng to do.
   – volunteer to co-ordinate in the regions, to contact activists in the area and to be the local distribution point.
   – let us know how much publicity material they would need.
   – raise some money to pay for the above. Cheques to . . .

   And we said we would:
   – inform them what other groups were doing and pass on suggestions for action, provided they sent them to us.
   – provide publicity material (a leaflet to encourage others to take part to give to local women's groups, trade unions).
   Later, balloons and T-shirts were also available.

I didn't have the contacts or knowledge to do this properly alone. My ability to outreach reflected my age, class, colour, interests and pocket so I failed to reach trade union women, or many working-class women, nor could I afford publicity on a large scale.

Putting the idea in *Sanity*, the CND journal, December 1981, resulted in an onslaught of mail: four or five letters every day for two months. They continued up to and beyond the day itself, in response to this one article! . . . moving, personal, funny letters – I was overwhelmed.

Some examples:
'May 24 is my 62nd birthday and being chairbound with arthritis, letter-writing is my best activity . . . I would like to send letters to women in Eastern Europe.'
'Please could you send me ideas of things I might do. I'm still in the Sixth and would like to do something in school. Living in Suffolk, with sited missiles and being the next generation, having my right to live and produce children and future life threatened, I feel I should do something to alter the things which I feel strongly about . . . I feel powerless and on my own . . . help me change this.'

– provide hints on how to contact local press (Draft press release).

Many women asked for *more* information and *who* was organising this, and *what* should they do? I was learning a lot by experience:

– that large-scale decentralised self-organised actions are a novel idea and no one (including myself) was quite sure how to organise them;

– that it was an appealing idea. Women were writing back who had never previously been part of any kind of action. Here suddenly was something you could be part of if you were wheelchair-bound, lived in the Outer Hebrides or had 'O' levels that day;

– that I had taken on far more than I could handle. I didn't even have the money to answer all the letters. None of the national organisations was very supportive.

I sent out a desperate letter via the Women's Peace Alliance stating my position.

Help arrived. Sue took on the horrendous task of making regional address lists, putting people in touch with one another. Margot turned her dining-room into an office, used her capital to pay our bills and her time and work to make the idea a reality.

L.J.

Tasks

Create central co-ordinating committee
Get together a group of individuals who can work happily together and can co-ordinate nationally and liaise with international groups.

We did not manage to get the hoped-for five people together – only two emerged. There are roles that could have been easily undertaken separately, e.g. liaison with international contacts. All our efforts would have been been greatly improved with more womanpower applied to each task. If you are co-ordinating nationally, it is impossible to initiate an event in your own neighbourhood.

Main Tasks
A. Networking – nationally/ internationally
B. Publicity material
C. Mailing
D. Fundraising
E. National media
F. Common Actions

A. Networking
Ask groups for information about what they are doing, make suggestions of what they might like to do, and circulate all this. We did this four times.

We also put as many women as possible in touch with others in their region. We asked for women to take on the co-ordinating in their regions.

The different ideas coming from all the women were endless, and encouraged them to suit the action to fit their area, talents and resources. As the political climate changed with the Falklands Crisis the type of event planned also changed, from festivals and fun to more serious 'drop-in for a chat', signatures for a cease-fire petition.

Sue, housebound in Wolverhampton, sent postcards to all our contacts with the names and addresses of others in the area.

About ten women said they would co-ordinate in their region, and the most important of these turned out to be Jo in

Wales, who had to translate the leaflets and posters into Welsh, and Fiona who struggled to co-ordinate Scotland, which is a story in itself!

B. Publicity Materials

What do you need? We produced posters, stickers for armbands, a leaflet introducing the idea of the day to women, a leaflet to give out to the public on the day, balloons with the logo, and T-shirts.

The most important thing is to have a good symbol or logo that can be shared by all and used on all materials.

We had a lot of trouble getting a good poster designed and and I'm not at all sure all the effort was worthwhile, because each group needed a poster/bill that suited its own event, e.g. Nottingham WONT's poster had to ask for plants to be taken to a certain spot to be planted at Molesworth Peace Camp, and why.

The initial introductory leaflet was essential and could have been more widely used; the general handout was also good, but could have been circulated and instant-printed locally to save parcelling and postage (and translated into Welsh).

The balloons and stickers were very popular although we did not sell them as moneymakers. They also gave women ideas for other publicity materials – such as buttons, badges, car-stickers, jewellery, etc. A cheap, cotton T-shirt would have been easier to sell.

C. Mailing

You need someone who likes doing this sort of job – working

This was the most tedious part of the whole organisation.

out who needs how many of what, packing up parcels that won't fall apart, and getting them all posted off.

It took me many hours rolling up hundreds of posters, parcelling up leaflets, sticking and tying. Luckily I have a very pleasant village post lady who spent the morning with me, weighing and sticking on stamps. A communal wrap-up would have been fun, but probably not as efficient as working on my own.

D. Where is the Money Coming From?

You need to prepare a rough budget, which in our case came to £1000 and worked out about right. Then you can send this budget to whoever you think might give you funds. The money does come in eventually, but the difficulty is starting with little.

Lynne subsidised the first part of the campaign with her own money, then Margot paid the bills for printing, postage, etc. In the end the money arrived in mainly small donations, but a properly arranged loan would have been more efficient and made planning and ordering materials easier.

You need enough security to launch out and order good publicity stuff – but not to go too mad or be over-ambitious.

E. The Media

Make a press list of all those you think worth contacting: monthlies, weeklies, national dailies and Sundays, radical, political, churches, women's. TV stations and radio stations, picking out any programmes worth special contact. Local groups can deal with local press, radio and television stations, but we sent them suggestions for getting into local media and a draft press release.

National media are very difficult to crack. All the different media have different schedules e.g. women's magazines work three months ahead, news programmes a week ahead. It really does need someone working on it, so she can get to grips with this and contact as many media people personally as possible. Feature articles need to be tailor-written for each journal, and this also takes time.

Send press releases to all the media; follow this up with one or two phone calls, and more press releases if necessary – a lot of time and energy. We also sent small 'pieces' to the Events columns of some journals.

After all the effort, we did not get much publicity – partly because all news was edged out by Falklands news. Sue worked really hard on the news media in West Midlands, but was balked at every turn – Pebble Mill at One finished that week for the summer, Birmingham had its first boy sailor casualty in the Falklands, Central TV was not interested, Radio Birmingham recorded an interview but didn't use it, independent radio promised an interview but then said they knew nothing about it. There was, as usual, better response from the local press.

F. Common Actions

The 'common' action we planned was a phone-in to government departments; we gave our contacts the names and telephone numbers for the Prime Minister's office, the Foreign Office, the Ministry of Defence and the Control and Disarmament Information Office. We allocated each region an hour in which to phone, starting from the South in the morning to Scotland towards evening, and also gave hints on how to leave a message.

The phone-in was very popular and the women soon realised that they *were* acting with others when the lines were engaged and the secretaries said they had been busy taking calls. Many women had long conversations, especially with the Arms Control Office, and were sent literature afterwards. This action was useful because anyone could take part if 'they could afford the phone charges or summon up the courage to do so' (Burgess Hill, Sussex), and it gave women the experience of talking direct to government officials.

International

Try and convey to all groups that things are happening internationally, e.g. by circulating messages of goodwill.

Telegrams would have been nice but too expensive. We reduced the messages to a sheet and sent them to coordinators.

Follow-up

Collect reports, articles for media.
Circulate all contacts with report and suggestions of how to continue action and maintain network.
Evaluate day!
Take a rest.

We suggested that women maintain their local groups if newly started, and join the Women's Peace Alliance to keep in touch.

M.M.

The Day Itself

Some 90 different events took place on 24 May all over Britain, in all shapes and sizes, from one schoolgirl wearing an armband into school exams to a full-scale procession through the city with a float; and a big public rally with well known women speakers. Market stalls in town squares, vigils, street theatre and so on took place all about the country. Most of the events were comparatively small, but all involved peace women meeting and talking to their neighbours and fellow citizens. Everywhere questions were raised about the Falklands crisis. In Bath people queued to sign a petition calling for a ceasefire. In my own village, where Elaine, not previously involved in the peace movement, organised a peace prayer service in the church, there was a lot of discussion and controversy stirred up as to whether this service should take place. Leaflets were delivered to all 60 houses in the village and 25 came – and every week we continue our peace service, and the arguments carry on too.

M.M.

International Events
From Holland on 24 May:
Hallo! . . .
Thanks a lot for sending some of your material. It's beautiful. Here is some of ours for you. Lots of things are going to happen

here! Including something like Greenham Common – a women's peace camp begins today at Soesterberg.

From France:

We are organising a demonstration in front of the Pompidou Centre in Paris. On the 24th there will be different activities in many French cities – Lyon, Marseille, Toulouse, Chateauroux, Rennes, Carpentras, Alsace.

From Norway:

Here in Norway women in every county are organising peace-actions. . . A new poster has been made for the day by the artist Kari Rolfsen (the future of two playing children). In Oslo eleven action centres are set up to distribute information. A quiet children's march will go through the central city ending at the concert hall, where a peace concert will end the day.

From Crete (Bee from Norwich):

I sent off, from the abandoned Venetian fort at the southern point of Paleochera, three balloons with doves holding olive branches (bought in the local store), one in each direction, each with a label attached, explaining the day.

Evaluation

It is possible to have a decentralised European action with only tiny resources, and reach many women who would not take part in mass demonstrations in centres of government.

These women in their turn meet, talk and leaflet the people in their own community, who are probably more impressed by this approach than by a couple of minutes on the television news.

One woman or a small group of women can organise a *big* local event in a small way; in Britain, with 90 events all over the country, there were 500 women involved in organising instead of a handful in a central office.

It is very difficult getting the national media to take notice!

'We found the Day a really good focus for our efforts – having been sitting around talking for some months, the commitment we'd made to do something on 24 May shook us into activity and the group has become larger and stronger as a result.'
(Pat – Lancaster WONT)

'The turn-out was quite high, 100–150. I feel I gained maximum publicity – a radio interview, large photograph and report in the *Evening Argus*, a big front page write-up in local press. Considering I was the sole organiser, I feel I did very well.
(Lynda, Lancing, Sussex)

Children in Woodstock make a dove collage, Women's Day for Disarmament, 24 May 1982

But this kind of event is *excellent* for local news.

Coordination is hard work: (One woman can handle 200 contacts by hand – just. Office machinery, e.g. word processors etc, is needed for more.)

Cooperation established around such an action can have a lasting effect. The networks don't end with the day.

'We were quite pleased with our event in Leicester . . . 116 women bought and signed a paper dove to be sent to the Prime Minister. We took over £200 during the day to be sent to the peace camps . . . we all gained experience and contacts, and I made an environmental sculpture which worked very well. It was the first time I have been able to produce something for peace without being contrived – I was very grateful to be able to do this.'
(Anna – Leicester)

11
Organising a Mass Lobby of Parliament: Families against the Bomb

ANNE TUTTON

We came together as a group partly because some of us found it difficult to get out to evening meetings of CND, but also because many of us felt that as women bringing up children we had something special to give the peace movement, and that that 'something' wouldn't be tapped by more mainstream organisations. In addition, most of us felt inhibited about asserting ourselves at more formal meetings.

We are quite diverse in our backgrounds and lifestyles and in our political thinking, but we are all united in the emotions we feel around our children and the nuclear threat. We are all frightened – we are also angry. We felt right from the start that we wanted to channel these powerful emotions and put them to good use in effective action.

We met in the day (and continue to do so) at the home of one of us, bringing children with us. For a while one of us regularly undertook the running of the creche and then we tried to do it by rota; but with all the will in the world the creche doesn't always work and there are always small ones wandering in and out – and making their demands felt.

It took us a while to get around to deciding to organise the lobby. As a group we had tried going out to other women with small children, we supported local peace activities, we had education evenings; but what we really wanted to do was to make some sort of political statement and make it loudly.

One of us hit on the idea of a lobby and we had a meeting to discuss how we could go about it. This time it was an evening meeting – we really felt that it wasn't possible to concentrate properly with our vociferous youngsters around – and from then on we had evening meetings held in the home of one of the single parents amongst us. There was a lot of anxiety expressed at that first meeting, as to whether we could undertake such an enormous task as the organisation of a national lobby. But while there were some who felt very daunted by the prospect, there were also some who were almost wildly optimistic at that stage. As the Day grew nearer it seemed that our feelings about it reversed so that those who had been daunted became optimistic, and vice versa. But at all times there seemed to be one of the group who could inspire the ones who had begun to wilt: a sort of natural balance of energies.

How did we do it? The best way of explaining seems to be to set out the timetable we set ourselves, then describe the tasks. The women involved describe the tasks themselves.

The Timetable

Early November evening	Initial meeting to decide on what direct action we could take – decided to organise lobby of parliament.
One week later – day meeting	Put idea to rest of day group, asked who wanted to be involved, explained what we thought it would involve, stated it would mean a commitment of one evening a week.
One week later – evening meeting	We divided the seven people present into three areas initially: fund-raising, publicity and contacts.
21 November	First fund-raising event: a jumble sale and auction which raised £300.
November – Xmas	Approached CND for money. They agreed we could use their stationery and mailing facilities. Wrote to charitable trusts. Began asking people to speak at public meetings. Began putting together mailing list – groups, organisations, individuals etc. Began asking well known people for their support. Began writing to MPs asking them to speak in Grand Committee Room. Asked Joan Maynard to be main support MP.
22 December	Press aspect discussed with freelance journalist. Central Hall, Westminster, finally booked after

	several attempts to find suitable place for public meeting.
Xmas	Two fund-raising parties.
Early January	Met with Margaret Cohen (who helped organise Nursery School Lobbies in 70s) for advice. Wrote first press release – made list of publications to send it to, using *Using the Media*, and sent it out. Went to see Westminster Ceremonials Police.
16 January	Sent out Mailing 1, using CND facilities: telling women that we were planning to lobby and why. Enclosing tear-off slip on which to register interest, name of constituency, etc.
End of January	Started inviting public figures to speak at public meetings.
3 February	Went to see Joan Maynard MP.
13 February	Held fund-raising classical concert. Raised £200.
Mid February	Ex-press officer for NUT helped with press contact list and offered to write second press release.
20 February	Held benefit gig. Raised £200.
Throughout February	Mailing 1 sent out.
1 March	Started thinking about children's entertainment and Rhondda offered to help.
4 March	Meeting with Joyce Gould of Labour Party for advice.
Mid March through to end of March	Song composed for lobby by sympathetic songwriter. Leaflets printed Sent out Mailing 2, asking people to distribute leaflets and write to MPs, either making appointment for 18 May or expressing views if unable to go. Draft letters enclosed with leaflets. Booked room at House of Commons for Press

	Conference.
	Sent letters to MPs.
	Started work on Briefing.
	Gained Sue W. to organise the stewards.
5 April	Started organising timetable for speakers in Central Hall.
Mid April	Decided to give budget to person working with children's entertainment.
	2nd press release discussed and written.
25 April	Meeting with TGWU member experienced in stewarding.
	3000 posters printed.
	3000 balloons ordered.
	2nd visit to Ceremonials Police.
End of April	2nd press release sent out.
	Organised St John's Ambulance.
	Arranged insurance cover – visited Central Hall to check it out.
	Entertainers booked for children's room.
29 April	Held social to inform rest of FAB what was happening and ask for help with stewarding, leafletting etc.
Early May	Sent out timetable to speakers.
	Briefing printed.
	Meeting with ex-press officer to discuss press conference, 3rd press release and statement for press.
	Started dove.
7 May	Rally organised by other local group. Press Conference invites sent out.
8/9 may	3rd mailing sent out with briefing, guide to lobbying and maps of Westminster area.
8 May	Fly-posting organised. Sending out last-minute posters and leaflets.
	Started rehearsing children for song.
10 May	Went to see Whips at House of Commons.
13 May	Held Press Conference at House of Commons.

	Sent out 3rd press release and FAB press statement.
16 May	Stewards meeting.
17 May	Rang round national papers, TV and radio newsrooms and picture desks. Held last evening meeting to clear up last-minute questions.

The Tasks

Finance
I am not 'good with money', am not confident when dealing with banks and officials and, I'm ashamed to admit, have never kept efficient personal accounts. I felt the responsibility weigh very heavily on me as soon as I realised that we were no longer dealing in tens but in hundreds of pounds – at some point well over a thousand. All decisions about money were made by the group and I simply carried them out and kept the group informed regularly of the state of our finances so that we could make realistic decisions about future expenditure. This need for accountability calmed me down and made me work out a clear system of accounts, so that all the outgoings and incomings were down on paper, and my estimates of our financial situation tallied – more or less – with the bank statement. Before the lobby I said I couldn't possibly look after the finances. What I gained from the experience is the knowledge that, given similar support and encouragement, I could certainly do it again. *Pauline Schiff*

Press
Working for six years as a secretary at Mirror Group Newspapers was an advantage in that I didn't feel diffident about approaching the news and picture desks, but a disadvantage in that I felt very cynical about the sort of response we'd get – I'd filed many a press release in a rubbish bin myself. It would perhaps have been better if I'd been a little more naive. In the end we got radio and television – but no national paper coverage except the *Morning Star*, much as I expected. I should have used the peace movement papers more. You need a telephone for this job. *Glynis Williams*

Contacts and Mailing
I concerned myself mainly with compiling the information that would need to be sent out to potential lobbyists, and working out a system and timetable for sending this information to all the people

Poster designed by Sue Ambrose

whose addresses we had on our card index. I built up this index from the names of all the women's disarmament organisations I could track down, as well as those of any individuals we thought worth contacting. The search for clarification of what a lobby involved – none of us had ever been on one – led to several visits to the police near the House of Commons to sort out the practical arrangements for the smooth running of the lobby. We sent out advice both tactical, e.g. exhortations to write to MPs, and practical, e.g. where to alight from your coach. The work was relentless, totally absorbing to the point of making me *less* productive, and produced much anxiety. I had to design the poster – what image should we present? Would the leaflets get out in time? Were the letters worded correctly? The lobby itself did not attract the thousands of people I had dreamed of. In spite of that, when I passed through the Central Lobby of the House of Commons which normally looks so impenetrable and austere, I saw it swarming with women and children so that MPs were having to pick their way through buggies and crawling babies. I found the sight so startling and so inspiring that I could not possibly regret all the effort and anguish of the past few months.   *Sue Ambrose*

Briefing and Speakers
Initially I was jointly involved in other tasks, but found myself doing little organising and mostly typing, so preferred to work alone on the briefing: getting the facts together on Cruise and Trident; and organising speakers.

I found it an exciting experience, writing letters to famous people and having telephone conversations with people I had only previously read about or seen on TV. All the speakers without exception were friendly and helpful. The only real problem in the organisation, after 14 speakers had agreed to speak, was working out the timetable. This soon fell into place when each person expressed their preference for speaking at the afternoon or evening meeting.

The briefing caused me much anguish and was very difficult to write. In the beginning I had no idea what to include or exclude and did not know enough details about the weapons. So I had a lot of research to do and talked to a lot of people, including my husband who was very helpful. Eventually I came up with a paper and sent it to a member of our local CND to comment on. I also sent it to an expert, who didn't reply. I received some very useful comments from the member of CND and after some more group discussion the final paper was passed.   *Maggie Weatherby*

The Children's Song (publicity stunt)
We were sent a song 'Save Our Beautiful World', written especially
for the lobby, from a musician who lives in Worcestershire. The
words were extremely moving, and particularly apt to be sung by
children, who grouped themselves around a model dove, symbol of
peace:

> Listen to our small voice,
> You really have the choice
> Don't you know, it's not too late,
> To save our beautiful world.

Without this we would have had little media coverage.
Anne Wiggins

Stewarding
As a complete novice at stewarding, let alone the complexities of a
mass lobby of Parliament, my first objective was to find someone
with experience for advice. In addition I attended the UNA disarmament lobby, which provided me with a valuable pre-run and
enabled me to view the whole event as a consumer.

The task of stewarding could be broken down as follows:

(*a*) assembling a list of volunteers
(*b*) liaising with the Police (both the Ceremonials Branch of the
       Metropolitan Police and the in-House Police), the Whips at the
       House of Commons and the staff at Central Hall
(*c*) familiarising myself with the geography and facilities at Central
       Hall, the Houses of Parliament and the route between
(*d*) briefing the stewards shortly before the lobby (we produced a
       written guide and held a meeting) and allocating the positions
(*e*) on the day being available to check that the system was working
       smoothly and to make any on-the-spot decisions.

Since ours was a women's and children's lobby, our major problem was a logistical one of getting large numbers of small children
and pushchairs (and parents) through the Houses of Parliament and
its numerous flights of stairs. The police took this problem seriously
and we ensured that we had able-bodied personnel to help at all the
stairs. At the end of the day the police and Whips said that although
it had indeed been chaotic in the lobby (one of our aims after all was
to provide an impact), it had been well ordered chaos.

As the day approached I was aware of the fact that my mind was
so tied up with the lobby most of the time that my family was

inevitably aware of this, at times resentful and, in the case of my three-year-old, a bit insecure. However, I felt it was important to involve them where possible, so my children accompanied me to the two meetings at Westminster (much to the amusement of the other adults present). Overall the lobby was an educative and perhaps even an enriching experience for my chidren as well as myself. It has certainly added a new dimension to their play which now includes games like 'having a FAB meeting' and 'going to the Houses of Parliament'. *Sue Wilkie*

MPs

This was really a very straightforward task. It just involved writing to sympathetic MPs in order to gain their support and to ask them to publicise the lobby in their constituency and gain support for it there. Joan Maynard gave us advice and booked the Grand Committee Room and the room for the Press Conference. All the MPs I approached were sympathetic – some were very encouraging indeed – one local MP, Reg Race, was particularly helpful. It did make us aware, though, how few women MPs there actually are in Parliament. *Anne Tutton*

Children's Entertainment

The general plan was to provide entertainers throughout the afternoon, and have other activities on hand, such as colouring and cutting, to keep the children occupied.

Points to note: you need some capital, £100 in our case, as many entertainers can't work for free in the summer. Have a large space. Borrow a climbing frame or equivalent. Computer printout paper and crayons are useful. You also need a microphone for the entertainers if possible, to overcome background noice. Advertise the fact that all this is provided. We *didn't* and it would have made a lot of difference to many mothers coming a long way. *Rhonda*

Organising a gig

I enjoyed doing this, even with no previous experience. Book a hall and get a date fixed before approaching suitable bands. Have capital to *invest*. Screenprint posters, find volunteers to cook food to sell at the event, and others to steward, sell tickets, etc. Publicise it well.

Distributing posters

In contrast, this was difficult from start to finish. We didn't decide *how* we were going to do it before ordering large numbers of posters, so three weeks before the lobby we had 8000 leaflets and 3000 posters and no way of getting them out. It was too short notice for the national organisations to help. After hundreds of exhausting phone calls and frantic parcelling, I did succeed. However, many just sat in members' houses. No one was very keen on fly-posting – a good way of getting publicity.   *Pauline Miller*

Conclusion

Although we were thinking all the time of how to encourage more local women to become involved, our organising group remained small. This meant that as the date of the lobby came nearer and the work load increased, we became more exhausted and pressurised. There were things we did wrongly or neglected to do. It put a strain on our families and sometimes on our relationships with each other. It was a very difficult time.

The group didn't always function well. Some members felt we spent too much time on media coverage and the organisation of the day itself, and not enough on the needs of the women who were coming, and that emphasis had wrongly changed from a women's to a mass lobby. For instance, the wording on the poster changed from WOMEN OF BRITAIN SAY NO to COME AND MAKE YOUR VOICE HEARD. One member, unhappy with the lack of discussion about these things, did leave us and another has decided to play a less active role, but there is a togetherness about the remaining members – and the feeling of having survived a storm.

Why a lobby anyway? And why put the emphasis on it being a women's lobby when we are '*Families* Against the Bomb'?

We wanted to do something that would make a mark and we wanted to do something politically effective: the vision of hundreds of women with their children inside the hallowed chambers of the House of Commons lobbying their MPs seemed to fit the bill. We were also aware of the growing voice of women about the nuclear issue all over the country and we thought that a national lobby could draw together some of those voices – it allows each group its diversity while at the same time giving a common focus.

As to making it predominantly a women's lobby – this has created confusion among other groups, ourselves and our partners. We call ourselves 'Families Against the Bomb' quite simply because there is no other word that includes our children, on whose behalf we came together and who have become involved themselves in the campaign. Some of the group have partners who have become very supportive: but to call ourselves 'Parents and Children Against the Bomb' could exclude those partners who aren't parents and those who are in gay relationships. The word 'family' can embrace all.

We have had a lot of criticism, often from feminist groups, about calling ourselves 'families'. The ground for these objections has never been quite clear, unless it is the concept of a family as nothing more than a nuclear family, an isolated unit of mother/father/children. Surely, by clinging to this definition of a family, such critics are helping to perpetuate that concept. For me a family is a network of people who give each other mutual warmth and support, and working with the other women in the group so closely has meant that those are exactly the feelings that have emerged. And that caring – that love – is surely what it's all about anyway.

There are some very supportive men in the group, but it has been women who have initiated action, organised and been responsible for the work towards the lobby. The fact that we don't exclude men doesn't conflict with the fact that as women we feel it is time for women to find their voice on an issue about which they have until recently not been heard. We feel it is time for a more feminine perspective to come to the fore: we feel that it is urgent and imperative that it does. This doesn't have to exclude men of course, but it does mean that women must be given space to find their voice and then use it. That is why we decided we would make it a *women's* lobby.

And women did come, in their hundreds with their children – with their men or on their own. They came from all over the country and queued for ages outside the House of Commons – not an easy task with fretful children – and then waited again inside the Central Lobby for MPs, some of whom wouldn't come out to see them. So they then wrote letters to explain why they had come. At the end of the day we all felt that it was the lobbyists who had had the hardest job of all, and who of course made the day successful. We, as a group, did no more than create a space for those women (and their men and children) to voice their feelings. We hope that other groups of women will go on doing that all over the country – all the time – so that our pressure becomes too fierce to ignore or resist.

12
Campaigning Notes 1:
Networking, and Working in Groups

There are many excellent practical guides to campaigning for peace. They are listed in the Resource section. What follow are practical descriptions of processes and actions mentioned in the preceding chapters, many of them techniques developed by the groups concerned.

1: NETWORKING

Many women organise separately because they dislike the hierarchical and bureaucratic forms of the mixed organisations. Needless to say any successful and growing group needs to communicate, and sometimes act jointly. Women's Pentagon Action and Dutch Women for Peace present two ways of organising on a large geographical scale. The Dutch Women and Nottingham WONT also use telephone trees and explain how they work.

*Structure and Decision-making for Regional Women's Pentagon Action Groups (Ynestra King and Donna Gould)
We have a decentralised decision-making process which emphasises the autonomy of local WPA groups and the importance of local input into decisions about regional undertakings. 'Region' refers to the northeast US, the area we organised for the first Pentagon action. We discussed and rejected the idea of 'going national' because we felt that we would not be able to keep the democratic, participatory decision-making we value if we were a national organisation. 'Locals' are groups of women living close enough to be able to meet and work together on a regular basis.

The region is defined as a network of local groups which are autonomous and are responsible for financing their own operations.

*Established: Amherst, February 1981, Philadelphia, July 1981

Locals come together in a regional meeting when there is sufficient interest by the locals in some proposal for a collective activity for the whole region. Or locals might decide to meet together for some other reason – to evaluate a regional action, to exchange information about local work, to discuss some particular issue, etc. It was suggested at one point that we meet twice yearly in any case, but this suggestion has not be pursued.

The decision to undertake a collective action for the whole region (such as a demonstration, conference, etc.) *is made by a process which ensures real input from the locals.* Such an activity would be suggested by a local group who would sound out other locals and, if there is sufficient interest, pass its suggestion round by mail. If there is enough interest on the part of the locals, the initiating local will call a regional meeting. An agenda for this meeting will be sent to the locals enough in advance for them to be able to have a thorough discussion of the proposal prior to the regional meeting. If all the locals agree to the proposed activity, it will be a Women's Pentagon Action activity and carry that name. Other actions sponsored by a local or locals will be so identified. If there is a serious question or ambivalence about the proposed activity at the regional meeting, *it will go back to the locals for further discussion.*

We realise we may need to make some decisions quickly without going through the regular process for consultation described above. For such situations we agreed to a procedure for making decisions by telephone which required consensus of a minimum of two-thirds of the locals.

To help us keep in touch with each other and consider proposals for collective activity, each local should designate one or more contact people, a list of contact people should be available to each local, and we should have a telephone tree for quick communication. (This last has never become a reality as far as we know.) We also need a regional newsletter, but we have yet to follow through on this decision.

Notes on Organisation (Women for Peace, Netherlands)

Decisions in all groups are taken by consensus: 'hard work, but worthwhile'.

Groups can act autonomously, they are not 'controlled' by a 'higher' group, as long as they make clear that they act as a group of Women for Peace, not for 'Women for Peace'.

Elites are avoided by trying to send different representatives to meetings.

Telephone Tree

Each circle in the diagram also acts as a telephone circle. A message can be initiated by any woman, e.g. A, who simply rings the next person in the circle, B, who rings C. The cirlce is complete when G rings A. If A finds that B is out, she rings C and keeps trying B for as long as possible. Because of the way the circles interconnect, messages can travel quickly to all the women in the organisation. It is best for simple clear messages, e.g. 'there is a demonstration tomorrow at 2 o'clock', or as a quick way of finding out people's views on something. It's no good for discussion. (*Dutch Women for Peace*)

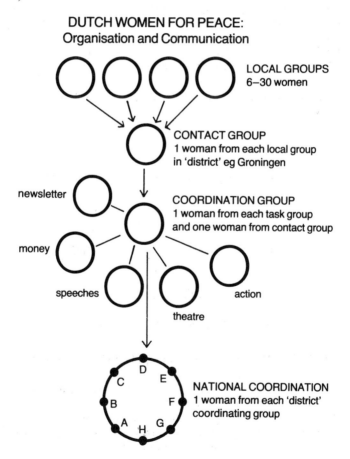

DUTCH WOMEN FOR PEACE:
Organisation and Communication

LOCAL GROUPS
6–30 women

CONTACT GROUP
1 woman from each local group
in 'district' eg Groningen

newsletter

COORDINATION GROUP
1 woman from each task group
and one woman from contact group

money

speeches

theatre

action

D E
C
B F
A H G

NATIONAL COORDINATION
1 woman from each 'district'
coordinating group

Small Telephone Tree for WONT groups in Britain
(Nottingham WONT)
What is described here is not a tree with a trunk but a circle. It's more democratic as anyone can start it at any given point. It also contains a check point to make sure that the message has got round everyone.

Each WONT group gives two contact phone numbers. It's best that they are ones where someone is usually in. When a message is received, the contact phones the next two towns (groups) in the circle. As there are two numbers for each town, it should be possible to get through. They will then phone the next two towns and so on. By this method each town will receive the same message twice – from the town before it and the town before them. This means there shouldn't be any breaks in the circle, as so often happens. Once the contact who initiated the message receives it back, she knows it's gone round and will stop it going round twice.

Small telephone tree for WONT groups in Britain

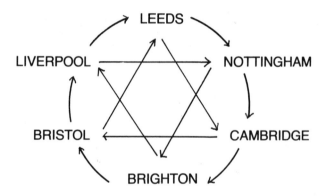

(NB Each town has *two* contact numbers)

2: GROUP PROCESS AND STRATEGY PLANNING

Nottingham WONT is one of the groups that give deliberate attention to both these areas. They answered my request for brief comments with the reply that they couldn't possibly be summarised and that they themselves used the books mentioned in the resource section. However, they gave an example of one of the tools they use in strategy planning.

The Social Speedometer

One of the aims of Nottingham WONT is to reach out to other women and to get them involved in peace campaigning. We use a tool called the social speedometer to help identify different groups

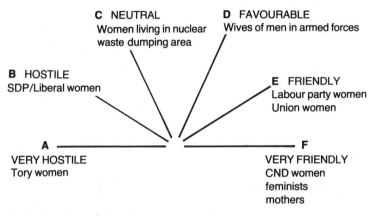

SOCIAL SPEEDOMETER
as used by Nottingham WONT to map
various womens' attitudes to campaign

C NEUTRAL
Women living in nuclear waste dumping area

D FAVOURABLE
Wives of men in armed forces

B HOSTILE
SDP/Liberal women

E FRIENDLY
Labour party women
Union women

A
VERY HOSTILE
Tory women

F
VERY FRIENDLY
CND women
feminists
mothers

Later in campaign –

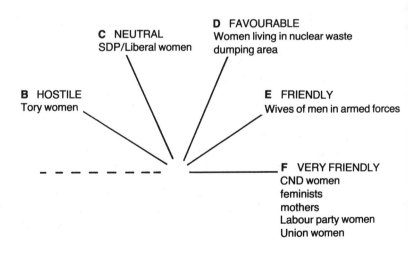

C NEUTRAL
SDP/Liberal women

D FAVOURABLE
Women living in nuclear waste dumping area

B HOSTILE
Tory women

E FRIENDLY
Wives of men in armed forces

F VERY FRIENDLY
CND women
feminists
mothers
Labour party women
Union women

of women in the community, and to assess each group in relation to our campaign. We plotted out the social speedometer (see diagram) and placed in appropriate categories different groups of women: we then plotted out the position of the groupings as they might be later on in our campaign. From making this analysis of women's involvement (or not), we could decide on actions that would shift one group along in the right direction (clockwise) or affect everyone.

Though we found it hard to categorise everyone, it was a useful exercise because it raised and helped answer the following:
– Who is the proposed action for?
– Will it be effective in making them more sympathetic and supportive of us?
– Are the hostile groups small or large in numbers?
– What would be the effect of an action that moved groups A and B anticlockwise, if all other groups moved clockwise? Would this polarising discredit them?

We found this a helpful tool in 'visualising' where we were trying to go.

Consensus Decision Making
Almost all the women writing this book acknowledge using this method to reach decisions whether consciously or unconsciously. It therefore seems worth explaining the method. (These notes are taken from *The 14 June Civil Disobedience Campaign Handbook*, New York, 1982)

What is Consensus?
Consensus is a process for group decision-making. It is a method by which an entire group of people can come to an agreement. The input and ideas of all participants are gathered and synthesised to arrive at a final decision acceptable to all. Through consensus, we are working not only to achieve better solutions, but also to promote the growth of community and trust.

Consensus vs. Voting
Voting is a means by which we choose one alternative from several. Consensus, on the other hand, is a process of synthesising many diverse elements together.

Voting is a win or lose model, in which people are more often concerned with the numbers it takes to 'win' than with the issue itself. Voting does not take into account individual feelings or needs. In essence, it is a quantitative, rather than qualitative, method of decision-making and may result in disaffected minorities who withdraw their support.

With consensus, people can and should work through differences and reach a mutually satisfactory position. It is possible for one person's insights or strongly held beliefs to sway the whole group. No ideas are lost, each member's input is valued as part of the solution.

What Does Consensus Mean?

Consensus does not mean that everyone thinks that the decision made is necessarily the best one possible, or even that all are sure it will work. What it does mean is that in coming to that decision, no one felt that her/his position on the matter was misunderstood or that it wasn't given a proper hearing. Hopefully, everyone will think it is the best decision; this often happens because, when it works, collective intelligence does come up with better solutions than could individuals.

Forming the Consensus Proposals

During discussion a proposal for a resolution is put forward. It is amended and modified through more discussion, or withdrawn if it seems to be a dead end. During this discussion period it is important to articulate differences clearly. It is the responsibility of those who are having trouble with a proposal to put forth alternative suggestions.

The fundamental right of consensus is for all people to be able to express themselves in their own words and of their own will. The fundamental responsibility of consensus is to assure others of their right to speak and be heard. Coercion and trade-offs are replaced with creative alternatives, and compromise with synthesis.

When a proposal seems to be well understood by everyone, and there are no new changes asked for, the facilitator(s) can ask if there are any objections or reservations to it. If there are no objections, there can be a call for consensus. If there are still no objections, then after a moment of silence you have your decision. Once consensus does appear to have been reached, it really helps to have someone repeat the decision to the group so everyone is clear on what has been decided.

Difficulties in Reaching Consensus

If a decision has been reached, or is on the verge of being reached, that you cannot support, there are several ways to express your objections:

Non-support ('I don't see the need for this, but I'll go along'.)
Reservations ('I think this may be a mistake, but I can live with it.')
Standing aside ('I personally can't to this, but I won't stop others from doing it.')
Blocking ('I cannot support this or allow the group to support this. It is immoral.' If a final decision violates someone's fundamental moral values they are obligated to block consensus.)
Withdrawing from the group. Obviously, if many people express non-support or reservations or stand aside or leave the group, it may not be a viable decision, even if no one directly blocks it. This is what is known as a 'lukewarm' consensus and it is just as desirable as a lukewarm bath.

If consensus is blocked and no new consensus can be reached, the group stays with whatever the previous decision was on the subject, or does nothing if that is applicable. Major philosophical or moral questions that will come up with each affinity group will have to be worked through as soon as the group forms.

Roles in a Consensus Meeting
There are several roles which, if filled, can help consensus decision-making run smoothly. The *facilitator(s)* aids the group in defining decisions that need to be made, helps it through the stages of reaching an agreement, keeps the meeting moving, focusses discussion to the point at hand, makes sure everyone has the opportunity to participate, and formulates and tests to see if consensus has been reached. Facilitators help to direct the process of the meeting, not its content. They never make decisions for the group. If a facilitator feels too emotionally involved in an issue or discussion and cannot remain neutral in behaviour, if not in attitude, then she should ask someone to take over the task of facilitation for that agenda item.

A *mood-watcher* is someone besides the facilitator who watches and comments on individual and group feelings and patterns of participation. Mood-watchers need to be especially tuned in to the sexism of group dynamics.

A *recorder* can take notes on the meeting, especially of decisions made and means of implementation, and a *time-keeper* keeps things going on schedule so that each agenda item can be covered in the time allotted for it (if discussion runs over the time for an item, the group may or may not decide to contract for more time to finish up).

Even though individuals take on these roles, all participants in a meeting should be aware of and involved in the issues, process and feelings of the group, and should share their individual expertise in helping the group run smoothly and reach decisions.

Attitudes and Behaviour which Help a Group Reach Consensus

Responsibility: Participants are responsible for voicing their opinions, participating in the discussion, and actively implementing the agreement.

Self-discipline: Blocking consensus should be done only for principled objections. Object clearly, to the point, and without putdowns or speeches. Participate in finding an alternative solution.

Respect: Respect others and trust them to make responsible input.

Cooperation: Look for areas of agreement and common ground, and build on them. Avoid competition, right/wrong, win/lose thinking.

Struggle: Use clear means of disagreement – no putdowns. Use disagreements and arguments to learn, grow and change. Work hard to build unity in the group, but not at the expense of the individuals who are its members.

13
Campaigning Notes 2: Action

PLANNING ACTION

(*a*) Ten steps to Organising a Short Walk (Jini Lavelle)

Having decided on the nature of the event and the date:

1. Contact local authority (city engineers or parks) for permission to use public areas.

2. Contact police for permission to march and to confirm the route to take through the town. It is best to go to the Chief Inspector with a plan of where *you* want to march. He will then liaise with the local authority and arrange for police support on the day.

3. Arrange a 'public liability' insurance policy. This should cover accidents during the walk or in the park or any damage to park property for about £13 for the day. A copy of this document will be required by the legal department of the local authority. Any local accident and insurance company will arrange the policy.

4. Book the entertainment well in advance, as many entertainers are booked up months before, particularly for week-ends.

5. Publicity:
Posters (1000 in two colours, approx. £100 at 1982 prices)
Leaflets (10,000 black and white, approx £45 at 1982 prices)
Car stickers, Badges, T-shirts, hand-outs, printed balloons, etc.
Printing takes from one to two weeks, designing and wording a lot longer!
Final artwork, layout, lettering, etc. should be done by a professional.
Some printing firms will do artwork at additional cost.

6. Finance:
Raise money through sponsorship – peace groups, Trade Unions.

NB special interest groups such as childbirth lobbies etc. Collect on the day. Sell badges/balloons etc. Hold fund-raising events.

7. Media:
Try hard (see details in other action plans).

8. Publicity distribution:
Get volunteers; we needed 100 to do poster distribution. Leaflet area of event one week before. Fly-post immediately before.

9. Provide in park:
Hot food from mobile catering van
Literature stall
Public address system if possible
Handout about yourselves/aims, etc.

10. Have a nice Walk!

(b) Organising Peace March à la Women-for-Life-on-Earth (Anne Pettit and Linnie Baldwin)

Getting a long-distance march together does not need super-human capabilities. WFLOE 1 was organised from a rubble-strewn room with a telephone and address book: WFLOE 2 was coordinated by Linnie who also had a full-time job.

You need at least three months.

You need two or three others who show interest. Between you, you need a telephone, preferably a car and a big diary/address book.

1. Get yourselves together with maps and calendars and sort out a rough idea of *route and dates*. Also theme/title of march. Before you fix route and dates, float the idea with a few phone calls or visits to some of the groups you will be asking for help. If the response is on the whole favourable, you can cope with some tepid responses by avoiding those places or finding other people to deal with.

Twelve miles a day is a reasonable average. A smallish (under 100) march moves at about 2½–3 miles an hour, with pushchairs. CND can supply information about military installations and US bases.

2. As soon as route and date are sorted out, print a basic inform-ation leaflet with sketch map of route. Get an attractive poster made – as many as you can afford. Send posters and leaflets to anyone you think might be sympathetic – groups and individuals.

Write down every contact. CND have lists of all local groups and affiliated organisations. Send information to women's monthly magazines and Woman's Hour because they plan three months in advance.

3. *Money* Duplicate a letter asking for donations and send to local trades councils, trades union branches, political party branches, churches, WIs and anyone else you can think of, or suggest they sponsor a marcher. Try CND for a float. We asked each marcher to send £10 in advance and this paid for some of our phone bills, printing costs and mailing. The rest was recouped from collection along the route.

4. *Overnight stops* Need not be the main towns. Staying in small towns and villages could have three advantages:

(*i*) You'd be walking through the towns in the middle of the day when there are people around, instead of always arriving at 5 p.m. as the shops shut and leaving before 10 a.m. before it gets busy.

(*ii*) Smaller places can provide a pleasanter atmosphere for relaxing and meeting in the evenings. If marchers bring tents you could camp.

(*iii*) The march and any evening events are more of an 'excitement' in a small place than in a large one: you may meet and talk to more people in a village hall meeting than you would in a big town. Every village in Britain has at least one village hall and statistically at least half a dozen peace movement sympathisers *who may not be organised as a group.* (After your march, they will be.) Have *one* reliable contact in each place where you will stop, to find accommodation. People may offer to provide food. That's great. You may have to cook your own. (We never did.) Your contact will also need to contact local St John Ambulance to come along and treat feet on the night, and contact the local press about you.

Lunch Stops There may be a local group, Labour Party group or church group who would like to do a lunch stop in a hall for you. This is a good way to get people involved who sympathise but don't normally do anything active for disarmament.

5. *Recruiting marchers* Obviously through notices in the peace magazines, etc. and through the local group network, *but* try and get outside it.

THE MORE MENTIONS IN THE NATIONAL PRESS YOU CAN GET, THE MORE INTERESTING A MIX OF PEOPLE YOU'LL GET ON THE MARCH. Both WFLOE marches have been starting-points for women previously uninvolved and outside the 'peace network'.

Duplicate a detailed leaflet to send to every would be marcher:

(*i*) where to go the night before it starts and the morning it starts;

(*ii*) route details for those wanting to join en route;

(*iii*) what to bring – clothes, how much money, sensible shoes, etc. and sleeping bag;

(*iv*) what they can expect in the way of accommodation, arrangements for children (if any) – people are more likely to come if they think it's well organised;

(*v*) what they can do to help – publicity in their areas, funding, and ideas, e.g. for motifs, banners etc.

6. *Numbers* Small may be beautiful. Under 50 is easy to accommodate and cook for, and feels like a group that can meet and listen and talk as a group. Expect 50–65 per cent of those who say they're coming to come.

7. *Police* Must be told. You will need police escort for your own and other road users' safety.

Write to Chief Constable of each police division you go through. Give details of times, road number, dates. A visit to your local police station may be useful. Be polite and firm. Reassure them that you'll have stewards. Verify all arrangements with a phone call the night before. Have a police liaison person who has an Ordnance Survey map on the march. Watch out! Police may try to route you round the outside of town.

8. *Transport* Transport will be needed to carry luggage. You may need to hire a van. At least two cars to accompany, one for general running about, the other as a life-support vehicle with a large boot. In the boot are First Aid Kit, elastoplast for feet, and cold drinks and paper cups. This car goes ahead and stops in a suitable place every two to three miles for ten-minute drink stops.

9. Get a leaflet printed to hand out along the route. (We got rid of 20,000 in ten days.) Simple wording; get the message clear. Explain who, where, why.

10. *Publicity* Write a Press Statement and send it to as many papers and individual reporters, programme producers you can garner. Send it one/two weeks ahead; three/four days ahead, ring them up. Add your drops of water on to the stones of the straight women's magazines.

11. Keep in constant contact by phone and visit with those organising hospitality/food/entertainments. Hold a meeting the night before in start-town to meet everybody coming. Don't forget collecting

boxes, banners, leaflets. Tear your hair out.

12. Try and have a nice send-off with a few local speakers, music.

On the March
Encourage singers and musicians to come. The Fall-Out Band can be contacted via CND. Sing! It works wonders.

Don't just give leaflets to people. Talk to them. Have a car behind to pick up those caught up in dialogues.

Leave on time and have a meeting just for marchers each night, if possible. If you want to hand in a letter at a Base or military installation, write to the Base Commander beforehand to say you're coming and give time for an appointment.

Make sure those who provide tea, food, etc. are thanked clearly and loudly. You are sowing the seeds of goodwill. Do not stamp on your seedlings by leaving village halls in an awful mess.

Try to get a video made of the march, including planning sessions, to take back and show to the people along the route, to water seedlings.

Have a 'health person' who watches out for those finding it hard going. Make sure they get a lift; or foot treatment, in time to stop bad blisters. Look after each other.

Circulate an *address list* of all marchers afterwards – this is network-building.

An alternative to walking from place to place could be to cycle, or even drive – perhaps a bus? – then you could spend *more* time in shopping centres and on streets talking to people.

(c) Setting up a Women-only Peace Camp (Waddington Women's Peace Camp)

1. Assemble a core group of like-minded women. Over several meetings discuss aims, develop trust and make practical plans. *Work collectively. You do not need a leader. New skills will be learnt as required to suit almost any situation.* Sort out a policy regarding male visitors; produce an overall policy statement to release to the press and visitors; work out individual commitments (e.g. time available per woman) – clarify this so that no woman feels pressure put on her to spend more time/energy at the camp than she is able to give.

2. Visit the proposed site unobtrusively after a base/nuclear power

station has been decided upon. View 'reserve' sites. Consider accessibility for campers and the public (e.g. public transport, travelling from home for members, etc.); consider very carefully the relative importance of the base from a military and strategic point of view (CND 'Activities' map is a good basic guide). Find an area as large as possible to camp, not too near houses because of the supposed 'health risk'. Look for grass or common land, but don't be put off by non-Utopian conditions.

3. Contact any women's groups and peace groups in the area – use discretion by talking to known contacts first. Local CND and peace groups may be offended if they are not given information at an early stage, but, for security reasons, it may be better to wait until the day you move in.

4. Consider basic facilities – sanitation and water. *Water* – if there is a fire hydrant nearby, you may be able to rent a stand pipe from the Water Board at a deposit of between £50 and £200. Alternative possibility – plastic water containers which a local supporter fills when required. *Sanitation* – try to find a manhole in which to deposit bodily waste. Otherwise use Elsan buckets, which can be emptied into a pit, but not Elsan fluid which is poisonous to the soil. One soak-away pit can be used for urine and small amounts of solids can be buried without constituting a health hazard. A public toilet may be available in the local village.

5. Gather/borrow basic equipment and money a few weeks beforehand so that anything faulty can be renovated and made serviceable. *Essentials*: several tents – at least one large tent; water containers; cooking facilities (Calor gas stove, etc.); Elsan buckets; blankets; sleeping bags; storable food; spades; lights (Tilly lamps/Hurricane lamps); a caravan, if possible, but not initially essential; warm clothing and wellingtons; plastic bowls; washing equipment; wood for fire and for carpentry; paint for graffiti/banners; a sign proclaiming who you are; leaflets to distribute to puzzled inquirers.

6. Find out whose land you are camping on from the Land Register in the County Council offices – whether it is County Council land, belonging to the Ministry of Defence or Ministry of Transport, or private or common land. Don't camp on private land without the permission of the owner or on MoD land (likelihood of speedy eviction).

7. Hire or borrow a van for moving in with female driver. Take as much support with you as possible, even if people cannot stay, so

that a large group can show initial solidarity and strength. *The first few hours are likely to be the most difficult as you may be asked to move.*

8. Plan arrival very carefully. Beforehand don't communicate by telephone. All move in together. Meet up a few miles from the base, but don't draw attention to yourselves by any overt behaviour (e.g. banners/stickers in evidence). Give each other strength and support – try to feel confident individually and in the group. You are in the right. Erect tents quickly. Don't be intimidated by the base police coming to question you. The Air Force police have no jurisdiction over civilians outside the base. Don't give *personal* names. Just carry on with the set plan of action. If local police are waiting, carry on until cautioned, then try and negotiate your position. It may be a good idea to have a woman with legal experience in your midst.

9. Find someone to act as a phone contact as soon as possible.

GOOD LUCK!!   IT'S NOT DIFFICULT!!

(d) Street 'Images' (Nottingham WONT)

Most campaigning groups when just formed want to do street theatre. It's a good way visually and orally of getting your message across, and makes more of an impression than leaflets which can just be thrown away. Street theatre is difficult though; it requires skills which are hard to learn. In our group it's always a bit beyond us, so instead we have developed what we call street images, or a street presence:

'Hiroshima Day'
Three of us coated ourselves with a mixture of flour and black powder paint, and with heads bowed and hands on the next one's shoulders, we stumbled through the streets of Nottingham. We carried a placard to inform people of how far radioactive dust travels, whilst others leafletted. Very effective.

Waste dumping
Needed:
    one person in a white coat with a very large red divining rod
    one person in a white coat with a drilling device
    one person in a white coat with a can of 'radioactive' waste material.
The three form a procession whose aim is to find a suitable place to

bury nuclear waste – outside shops, inside people's bags, in the main square. Other people are needed for leafletting.

When leafletting isn't allowed at an army recruitment show
Needed:
  two stretchers
  two dummies dressed in army uniform with plenty of bandages and red paint
  two signs, one saying 'I travelled to distant, exotic places, met unusual people and killed them'. The other saying, 'I travelled to distant, exotic places, met unusual people and got killed.'
  four people dressed as orderlies.
  People carry the stretchers with signs attached to them, very slowly around the area.

All the above take about one evening to prepare. Once you have the props you can repeat them over and over again. All we do is take one simple idea and mime it. Sometimes we incorporate a song – which can be pretty powerful. Whilst the action should get across the message in itself, it mainly should be a focus for leafletting – to make people want to find out more.

(*e*) Letter-writing

This appears to be something we are good at. It provided the starting point for German Women for Peace, and the basis for the Women's Day for Disarmament. Personal letters can also cross political divides in a way that other written propaganda cannot. Here's an example of women writing to women:

Dear Sister,
  We are happy to know that there are many Women for Peace in all countries. I hope that you are or will be one of them in your country.
  I wish you to know, that we in Norway and Nordic countries are deeply scared because of the weapons and bases in Europe, we have nightmares about what could happen to all of us.
  We will all feel safer, if your government as a member of the Warsaw Pact:
  – will refuse to be protected by weapons which may draw a holocaust upon everybody,
  – will call for the withdrawal of Warsaw Pact troops, weapons, bases and military stockpiles from your country,

– will demand that the government of the Soviet Union stop the development and production of nuclear weapons and agree with the government of the United States on a way of disposing of existing weapons.

Maybe you as a woman and citizen have already acted in order to put pressure on your government in this respect. I would be very happy, if you will let me know, what women are doing in your country.

But if you are not active yet, would you consider starting doing something about this?

We, Norway's Women for Peace press our government to:
– stop increasing the military budget since weapons cannot protect us anyway,
– protest officially against the arms race of the great powers,
– promote with all our strength the Nuclear Free Zone in Nordic countries and the nuclear disarmament in the whole of Europe from Poland to Portugal.

We have started this correspondence both within the country and outside the borders. We send letters directly to women in NATO countries and to the USA and the Soviet Union.

We, the women of all these countries, can unite our strength together against the insanity of the arms race.

We will not stay silent any longer.

WE DON'T WANT TO BE THE LAST GENERATION IN EUROPE.

WE DO NOT WANT TO BE EXTERMINATED BECAUSE OF THE MADNESS OF THE GREAT POWERS.

We, Women for Peace in Europe, let us all
– devote our strength to supporting our American and Soviet sisters in their demands for peace from their governments,
– force our governments to disarm.

With Peace greetings, yours
A Woman for Peace in Norway

SOME NOTES ON TAKING NONVIOLENT DIRECT ACTION (Lynne Jones)*

Non-violence, for most of the women in this book, is not just a tactic for action, but an approach to life, chosen because we are aiming for a non-violent society and believe that 'means determine ends'. Choosing non-violence may result in, but is not synonymous with, either direct action or civil disobedience. For instance, if your goal is ending nuclear power, turning off a light bulb to save electricity would be legal direct action. Occupying the site of the plant on a long-term basis to prevent construction would be illegal direct action. Trespassing briefly on the site would be illegal but symbolic, while going on a march to protest about it would be seen as legal and symbolic. They are all non-violent actions and may all play an important part in ending nuclear power.

Books and pamphlets listed in the resource section go into the philosophy and techniques of nonviolence in depth. The following are some points to consider if planning to take action, and an example of planning for one is the blockade at Greenham Common in March 1981.

Thinking of Action? Ask yourself:
Will it clarify the issues?
e.g. by blocking construction work on missile silos, we highlighted the fact that construction work was going on.
Do you have an attainable and significant goal?
e.g. a 24-hour blockade is long enough to cause inconvenience and show determination, while a long-term one may be difficult to maintain.
If the action results in direct confrontation, how would you deal with arrest? Violence? The threat of violence?
We feel that training greatly improves the way one deals with the above.
Will there be adequate support for such an action?
How will the media react? Local people?
Are you planning openly or secretly?
Secrecy is almost never total and can result in hierarchies between those who know and those who don't. Open planning results in trust, cooperation, possibly better plans and often support from surprising quarters.

*with help from Bee Pooley, notes by Diane Shelley, Region 2. *Direct Action Handbook.*

Do the positive gains of the action outweigh the losses?
Is it more important to spend a week or more in jail or be building another peace camp? Does getting arrested gain you more positive support than writing a leaflet?

Preparation for Mass Action. Blockade at Airbase.

(The blockade at Greenham was planned openly; and involved supporters coming from all over the country. The following would not be appropriate for small, local, possibly secret, actions.)

1. Non-violence training weekend should be held at least two months in advance at or near site, to enable potential participants to familiarise themselves with geography and learn skills they can take home to start local groups.

(*Note* Affinity groups: 5–15 people who know each other, are self-sufficient, and can take action together, form a good basis for non-violent direct action. Working in such a group prevents feelings of fear and isolation, provides a mutually supportive trusting atmosphere, facilitates decentralised decision making. The group can act autonomously and fulfil its own support needs. Groups *can't* form on this weekend, with people from widely dispersed geographical regions. They are best formed on a local basis.)

During weekend, go through plan of action. Role-play the whole thing. This will highlight deficiencies in plan, which can be remedied and give people an idea of how they might respond, intellectually, physically and emotionally, to action. Work on ways to improve responses.

Introduce people to group dynamics. How are they going to function as groups in action – making quick decisions? During confrontation? How is everyone in group going to feel supported and involved?

Sort out support roles necessary. What should groups provide for themselves? What functions can be centralised? e.g. the groups should look after their own physical needs: food, transport, etc.; provide their own legal observer. Press spokeswomen may be central. Emphasise need of support roles: they are not secondary – action cannot take place without them.

Have a legal briefing. Explain legal implications of action, arrest. How to deal with police. Explain role of legal observers. (Supporters who remain with but don't participate in action, and make notes of arrests, what happens, contact solicitors, act as witnesses in court, etc.)

2. Local training weekends: affinity groups form. Go through above. Work out how they will act, e.g. weave webs, sing, use chains. Who will do support? How will they deal with arrest? Non-cooperate? Bail solidarity? Refuse fines? Handle material needs – food, transport.

3. At Site of Action: Preparations
(*a*) Publicity
talk, leaflet, explain action to local community
press release
inform authorities, base personnel and police of intentions: what you intend to do, what special arrangements you are making, e.g. we let children and emergency vehicles through blockade.
(*b*) Support
Arrange legal support, friendly local solicitors to be available.
Arrange office base for liaison, press contact, legal contact for during and after action (in our case, a caravan at the camp and a telephone number in town).
Arrangements for sanitation (we had a Portacabin on site).
First Aid, childcare, transport, sleeping arrangements, food/drink ideally arranged by affinity groups but *don't* rely on this. Hall/ camping for sleeping.
(*c*) Practical preparations:
Write practical briefing. Explain action, how, why, where, when.
Legal details: solicitors' phone numbers, implications of arrest, what to do when arrested. List support roles group should fulfil, and those provided centrally. Map.
Mail to known participants.
Encourage everyone to come eight hours beforehand.
Write leaflet for public, to hand out on day.
Communication: Hire walkie-talkie (expensive) for widely dispersed action where groups can be isolated by police. Information can be relayed to central points. Cars/runners – less efficient.

4. Day Before
Ring media.
Set up central point for registration, communication, press liaison, transport.
Register all participants, supporters included, including phone number of person to be contacted if arrested.
Each group should go through practical briefing. Familiarise itself with site arrangements, food, etc.
NB Most participants in the blockade had done NO PREVIOUS

TRAINING and did not come in groups. EXPECT THIS. Arrange emergency training. We did two-hour sessions: people got into groups of ten – got to know each other, went through briefing, worked out decision-making process, support roles and ways of dealing with action, confrontation and arrest. (Pairing within groups also useful. Pairs share fears and anxieties, explain to each other how they are likely to react and how they would like partner to respond, stay together during action.)

Brief legal observers. We arranged for all legal information to go to central point, who then contacted solicitors – avoided duplication and clogging phones.

Brief press spokeswomen. Make sure every group has publicity leaflets, be prepared to telephone reports/speak to press through-out action.

Get together for final coordination.

Start action.

5. After Action

Follow up those arrested – bail, legal support.

Inform press of court dates, further plans.

All the participants need to come together in some way at the end of the action; closing ritual, song, a meal.

Evaluate action: what have we achieved? Learned?

We learned more from the action than the training, and something unexpected always happened. However, preparation beforehand makes participants feel secure and empowered, and improves the chances of good effective action.

We don't have to reinvent the wheel. There's a lot of experience around; read about it, learn from it.

Afterword

Like many of the women writing in this book, I, too, had one of those sudden moments of awareness. Sitting on a train two years ago, I was reading a pamphlet called *Protest and Survive* by E.P. Thompson. I'd bought it to while away the journey, but instead found the world closing in, with a sick sensation that there was no possibility of escape. So I did what seemed, to a doctor, the obvious thing, I joined the newly formed 'Medical Campaign Against Nuclear Weapons' and learned to give talks explaining the effects of hundred-mile-an-hour winds on soft human flesh; how difficult we find it just to deal with one burned child, let alone a hundred thousand; and in what slow and insidious ways radiation sickness kills a person. I found I could frighten people into action, and each talk left me utterly miserable and depressed, no matter how often I gave them. There had to be some other way than fear. Why is it in our society that we take the negative approach? I had spend six years in medical school learning not to rejoice in human life and health but rather to struggle with the process of disease. I was not expected to ask, what makes people well? but instead be fascinated by what makes them sick. So as a result I was better equipped to fight disease than to prevent it, and here in the peace movement the same pattern was being repeated. I wanted to find a way to reassert the positive, to say 'This is what life could be like, why don't we work for it?' It seemed to be women who were doing that, so I decided to work with women.

Editing this book has meant that I at last feel able to answer one question that bothers people. Should we organise separately? Isn't it divisive? I think not. Reading these stories one can see that separateness creates a space for talent, power and joy to emerge, that can only add to the peace movement, not detract from it. Are we frightened of diversity? It is the military after all who, in their desire for control through uniformity, are most threatened by it. Working in small groups we are developing skills that may strengthen all of us.

The other question is, of course, are we being effective? We are able to understand complex issues, mobilise in large numbers, take visionary action. Yet government policies remain unchanged. Is this because our representation in such policy-making bodies is minimal? There are two women in nuclear charge at the moment: Mrs Thatcher and Mrs Gandhi. There are no women in the upper echelons of NATO or the Warsaw Pact, one permanent woman representative on the UN Security Council, and very few involved in formal disarmament machinery. Should we be challenging this? Or is it the policy-making structures themselves that are inherently unsound? Should we be changing these?

It is essential to answer these questions because defining our aims will affect how we work. If it's important to get 'into power', we're going to have to learn skills that allow us to compete successfully, we're going to have to be single-minded and not allow personal feelings to get in the way. If on the other hand we define power in a different way, born from mutual cooperation, the ability to make connections, and acknowledge our feelings, we are going to have to change these power structures because we won't be able to function within them. The change itself becomes the solution. Unlike WPFS I don't think these approaches are compatible. WONT and WPA have followed this line of thought to the logical conclusion, acknowledged that change comes from the bottom up, and that it's a long struggle. The rest of us fudge the issue: perhaps in reaction to the 'political infighting' of mixed groups, perhaps because in a desire to emphasise the positive peacemaking side of our work, we want to avoid conflict at all costs.

I do not believe that peace is the absence of conflict but rather the ability to resolve conflicts without violence. We need to listen to each other, hear our differences and learn from them. We need to communicate in a network that is neither haphazard nor based on one ideological position. If we could find ways of working together that make us effective and allowed for our diversity in working for a common goal – a living earth – we might perhaps be closer to preventing those conflicts which threaten to destroy us all.

Lynne Jones, July 1982.

Resources

Books
There is now such a wealth of literature available on all aspects of the subject of Women and Peace, this can't hope to be a definitive list. It is simply a list of suggestions: both of books that make good starting points and some that are the main resources in their area. All those listed can be obtained from Housmans Bookshop or CND, unless specifically stated otherwise. Both the above will provide full booklists on request.

Women

Pioneers for Peace: Women's International League for Peace and Freedom 1915–1965 (Gertrude Bussey and Margaret Timms), WILPF 1980, available from them. £3.50.

Ain't Nowhere We Can Run: A Handbook for Women on the Nuclear Mentality (Susan Koen and Nina Swain) WAND 1980, £2.25. Excellent feminist introduction to Nuclear Technology and its dangers.

Nuclear Resisters (Feminists against Nuclear Power) P.D.C. available from above c/o Sisterwrite Bookshop, 190 Upper Street, London N1, Mail Order £1.25.

Testament of Youth and *Testament of Experience* (Vera Brittain) Virago £3.95 each. Moving autobiographical experiences of a feminist pacifist writer through First and Second World Wars.

Three Guineas (Virginia Woolf) Penguin 1977, 95p.

The Tamarisk Tree (Dora Russell – autobiography) Virago 1977, £3.50

Both of these last two books demonstrate that the connections made by feminists today are not new ones!

Campaigning

Peaceworking: A campaigning Handbook for Branches of UNA and other groups (Sandy Merritt) UNA £1.50. Practical advice on campaigning on all issues with which the U.N. is connected.

How to Get Rid of the Bomb: A Peace Action Handbook (Gavin Scott) Fontana, £1.95. A guide to using the democratic system to change government policy on Nuclear Weapons.

What Do We Do After We've Shown The Wargame? A Disarmament action manual (Dan Plesch) CND, £1.95. Campaigning handbook compiled with CND groups in mind.

Resource Manual for a Living Revolution (Coover, Deacon, Esser, Moore) New Society Press 1978, £7.95. A 'how to do it' book. Everything from constructing theories of social change to facilitating meetings, consensus decision taking, etc. Good for group process skills. American in orientation.

Cooperative and Community Group Dynamics . . . or Your Meetings Needn't be so Appalling (Randall, Southgate and Tomlinson) £1.50

Using the media: How to deal with the Press, Television and Radio (Denis McShane) Pluto Press 1979, £2.50

Nonviolence

The Politics of Nonviolent Action (Gene Sharp) Extending Horizon Books 1973, 3 vols. £2, £4, £4.85. Good lengthy introduction to history/theory/methods of nonviolence.

Revolution and Equilibrium (Barbara Deming) Grossman, N.Y., $3.95

Our Blood (Andrea Dworkin) The Women's Press 1982, £3.50. Both important writers on the connections between feminism and pacifism.

Introduction to Non-violent Action Training (Pamphlet by Dawn) 168 Railger Road, Dublin 6, 30p.

Hell No, We won't Glow (Sheryll Crown) Housmans, 45p. Practical pamphlet on taking action, based on actions at Seabrook Nuclear Power Plant, USA.

Organisers Manual (War Resisters League) WRL £2.50. Available from War Resisters International. Practical information on organising non-violent direct action, again based on experience in USA.

The Nuclear Arms Race

As Lambs to the Slaughter: The facts about Nuclear War (Paul Rogers, Malcolm Dando and Peter Van Den Dungen). Arrow 1981, £1.75. An examination of all the issues in clear factual up-to-date terms.

Nuclear Madness (Dr Helen Caldicott) Bantam 1980, £1.25. Looks at the whole nuclear fuel cycle in a straightforward, comprehensible way.

How to Make up your Mind About the Bomb (Robert Neild) André Deutsch 1981 £2.95. Well argued analysis of the risks and benefits of various disarmament strategies for Britain.

Protest and Survive (Eds. E.P. Thompson and Dan Smith) Penguin 1980, £1.50. Expanded version of original pamphlet with essays by Mary Kaldor, Alva Myrdal, and others.

Towards the Final Abyss: The State of the Nuclear Arms Race (Michael Pentz) J.D. Bernal Peace Library 1980, 30p. Good introduction to concepts of 'counterforce', lethality and other aspects of new nuclear weapons.

The Game of Disarmament (Alva Myrdal) Spokesman 1976, £4.25. The 'definitive' account of the arms race and militarisation in our world by Sweden's former Minister for Disarmament.

The Baroque Arsenal (Mary Kaldor) Andre Deutsch 1982, £7.95. Argues how the development of military forces, East and West, simply extrapolates past trends in more elaborate forms and how such forms endanger us whether or not they are used.

World Armaments and Disarmament SIPRI Yearbook 1981 (Taylor and Francis) 1981, £19.50. The definitive resource for facts and figures in the arms race. Expensive – borrow it.

The SIPRI Brochure, 80p. Summarises above.

World Military and Social Expenditures 1981 (Ruth Leger Sinard) World Priorities Inc., £2.25. Annual report containing summary and statistics comparing 141 countries by their economic, military and social indicators. Good discussion of world priorities, the nuclear power/weapons connections, gap between rich and poor nations, etc.

The Effects of Nuclear Weapons
The Medical Consequences of Nuclear Weapons (Prof. J. Humphrey, Dr M. Hartog, Dr H. Middleton) Medical Campaign against Nuclear Weapons 1981, 75p. Very good summary of medical effects.

Militarism
The Defence of the Realm in the 1980s (Dan Smith) Croom Helm 1980, £6.95. Critical analysis of Britain's defence policy in the 1980s.

On the Psychology of Military Incompetence (Norman F. Dixon) Futura 1979, £2.50

Loaded Questions: Women in the Military (ed. Wendy Chapkiss) Transnational Institute 1981, £1.95. A comprehensive starting point for any discussion on women and the military, including papers on the draft, and on the role of women in national liberation armies.

Arms Trade
Bombs for Breakfast: How the Arms Trade Causes Poverty, Repression and Militarisation. Committee on Poverty and the Arms Trade 1981, 75p.

Chemical Weapons
Rage Against the Dying: Campaign against Chemical and Biological Warfare (Elizabeth Sigmund) Pluto Press 1980, £1.95.

Nuclear Power
Nuclear Power for Beginners (Stephen Croall and Kaianders Sempler) Writers and Readers 1980, £1.95. A cartoon introduction!
Atoms for War: How Nuclear Energy Fuels the Arms Race (Howard Clark) CND 1982, 50p.

Civil Defence
The Cruellest Confidence Trick (Phil Bolsover) CND 1982, 80p. Shows how misleading government reassurance really is.
When the Wind Blows (Raymond Briggs) Hamish Hamilton 1982, £3.95. Comic book form – not a comic story – about a couple who were misled.

Psychology
Four Minutes the Midnight: The Bronowski Memorial Lecture (Nicholas Humphrey) BBC Publications 1981, £1.25. An explanation of the psychological mechanism we use to avoid facing the dangers of nuclear weapons.

Disarmament
Disarming Europe (eds. Mary Kaldor and Dan Smith) Merlin Press 1982, £3.60. Second half examines concrete proposals for disarmament such as alternative defence, nonalignment, etc.
Dynamics of European Nuclear Disarmament (Alva Myrdal and others). Spokesman 1981, £5.50. Essays by Rudolf Bahro, Robert Hayman and others.
A Short Guide to Disarmament (Alan Litterland) Housmans 1982, 85p.

General
The Fate of the Earth (Jonathan Schell) Picador 1982, £1.95

Hiroshima (John Hersey) Penguin 1981, £1.25. Classic account of what happened seen through the eyes of 6 'survivors'.

Nagasaki 1945 (Tatsuichiro Akizuki; translated by Keiichi Nagata, edited and introduced by Gordon Honeycombe) Quartet Books 1981, £2.50. The first full-length eyewitness account of the atomic bomb attack on Nagasaki, by a doctor working in one of the city's hospitals.

Unforgettable Fire Pictures Drawn by Atomic Bomb Survivors (Japan Broadcasting Corporation) Wildwood House 1981, £4.95. 'More moving than any book of photographs could be because what is registered is what has been burned into the minds of the survivors' John Hersey.

Periodicals

Various periodicals make good sources of up to date information.

SANITY – CND bimonthly – good way of keeping up to date with campaign in Britain.

Peace News. Fortnightly journal dealing with peace issues in the widest sense from a non-violent, feminist (usually) perspective: 3rd world militarism, the politics of health, nuclear technolgy . . .

Disarmament Campaigns. International monthly reports and articles.

END Bulletin. Bimonthly journal of European Nuclear Disarmament movement. Good mix of theoretical articles, activist reports with European perspective.

New Statesman, Scientific American, Financial Times are all good sources of information.

The Bulletin of The Atomic Scientists. Founded in 1945 by Hyman H Goldsmith and Eugene Rabinowitch, published by the Educational Foundation for Nuclear Science, Chicago, available from Walter C Patterson, 10 Chesham Road, Amersham, Bucks HP6 5ES.

Visual Materials

Many of the organisations listed in the address list have their own visual material available for loan. Contact them.

Films

These are four specially useful films. Concorde Films have many more. Organisations holding copies in brackets.

Critical Mass Videotape of talks given by Dr Helen Caldicott in Edinburgh, October 1980. Good on medical effects of nuclear fuel cycle and interesting discussion with women on what she thinks they can do. (Women for Life on Earth)

The War Game Pseudo-documentary depicting affects of nuclear attack on British town. The effect is devastating. (New up-to-date version being made.) (Concorde)

The Bomb British documentary looking at human implications of escalating arms race, tracing its development from Hiroshima to the present day. (Concorde)

"A Better Road to Peace" The viewpoint of the Ministry of Defence. (Central Office of Information)

Exhibitions

Sister Seven Exhibition of 20 posters, conceptual work/graphics/poetry/fiction, on an anti-nuclear theme. c/o Mary Michaels, 28 Carysfort Road, London N16 9AL

The Medical Effects of Nuclear War Available from Medical Campaign against Nuclear Weapons, 23A Tenyson Road, Cambridge.

Addresses

Organisations and Groups for Women

Babies Against the Bomb: c/o Tamara Swade, 50B Clevedon Mansions, Lissenden Gardens, London NW5.

Families Against the Bomb: 124a Northview Road, London N8

Oxford Mothers for Nuclear Disarmament: c/o 11 Warnborough Road, Oxford

Women's Peace Camp: RAF Waddington, Lincoln, Lincolnshire

Women's Peace Camp: USAF Greenham Common, Newbury, Berkshire

Women Oppose the Nuclear Threat (WONT): Natinal: Box 600, c/o Peace News, 8 Elm Avenue, Nottingham

Nottingham WONT: c/o Women's Centre, 32A Shakespeare Street, Nottingham

Women's Pentagon Action (USA): 339 Lafayette Street, New York, NY 10012

Women and Life on Earth (GB): 2 St Edmunds Cottages, Bove Town, Glastonbury, Somerset

Women for Peace (Federal Republic of Germany): Frauen fur Frieden, c/o Eva Quistorp, Bundesallee 139, D-1000 Berlin 41

Women for Peace (Netherlands): Vrouwen voor Vrede, PB 963, 3800 AZ Amersfoort, Netherlands

Women for Peace (Norway): c/o Romsted, Trudranqun. 12A, 1342 JAR, Norway

Japanese Women's Council for Shibakusae Women: 1-33-3 Hongo, Bunkyo-ku, Tokyo, Japan

Women's Peace Alliance: Box 240, Peace News, 8 Elm Avenue, Nottingham

Women's International League for Peace and Freedom: 29 Great James Street, London WC1N 3ES

Women for World Disarmament (UNA): North, Taunton, Somerset TA3 6HL

Liaison Committee of Women's Peace Groups: 25 Elsworthy Road, London NW3

Women's Party for Survival (now Women's Action for Nuclear Disarmament): PO Box B, Arlington, MA 02174, USA

The Women's Peace Alliance has many other addresses of Women's Peace organisations, both national and international.

National Organisations and Publications

Anti-nuclear Campaign: POB 216, Sheffield, Yorkshire S1 1BD

Bertrand Russell Peace Foundation: 45 Gamble Street, Nottingham, NG7 4ET

Campaign Against the Arms Trade: 5 Caledonian Road, London N1 9DX

Campaign for Nuclear Disarmament: 11 Goodwin Street, London N4 3HQ

European Nuclear Disarmament Campaign: 227 Seven Sisters Road, London N4 3HQ

National Peace Council (co-ordinating body for most British Peace Organisations): 29 Great James Street, London WC1N 3ES

War Resisters International: 55 Daws Street, London SE17 1EL

World Disarmament Campaign: 21 Little Russell Street, London WC1

(This is not a comprehensive list. There are numerous other Peace Groups – religious, special interest, etc. Contact National Peace Council for further information.)

Housmans Bookshop: 5 Caledonian Road, London N1

Sisterwrite Bookshop and Women's Research and Resources Centre: 190 Upper Street, London N1

Sister Seven: c/o Mary Michaels, 28 Carysfort Road, London N16 9AL

Concorde Films: 201 Felixstowe Road, Ipswich, Suffolk IP3 6BJ

Central Office of Information: films from Central Film Library, Chalfont Grove, Gerrards Cross, Bucks. SL9 8TN

Peace News: 8 Elm Avenue, Nottingham

Disarmament Campaigns: c/o Anna Poulownplein, 3, Postbus 18747, 2502 Es, The Hague, Netherlands

Sanity: c/o CND, 11 Goodwin Street, London N4 3HQ